CRISES OF ADOLESCENCE

Teenage Pregnancy:
Impact on Adolescent
Development

Report No. 118

CRISES OF ADOLESCENCE

Teenage Pregnancy: Impact on Adolescent Development

Formulated by the
Committee on Adolescence

Group for the Advancement of Psychiatry

BRUNNER/MAZEL *Publishers* • New York

Library of Congress Cataloging-in-Publication Data

Crises of adolescence, teenage pregnancy.

  (Report/Group for the Advancement of Psychiatry;
no. 118)
  Includes bibliographies and index.
  1. Pregnancy, Adolescent—Psychological aspects.
2. Adolescent parents—Mental health. 3. Adolescence—
Physiological aspects. 4. Pregnancy, Adolescent—
Economic aspects. I. Group for the Advancement of
Psychiatry. Committee on Adolescence. II. Series:
Report (Group for the Advancement of Psychiatry);
no. 118. [DNLM: 1. Adolescent Psychology. 2. Human
Development. 3. Pregnancy in Adolescence.
W1 RE209BR no. 118 / WS 462 C932]
RC321.G7 no. 118 616.89 s [155.5′33]   86-2304
[RJ507.A34]
ISBN 0-87630-426-9
ISBN 0-87630-427-7 (soft)

Copyright © 1986 by the Group for the Advancement of Psychiatry

Published by
BRUNNER/MAZEL, INC.
19 Union Square West
New York, New York 10003

All rights reserved. No part of this book may be reproduced by any process whatsoever without the written permission of the copyright owner.

MANUFACTURED IN THE UNITED STATES OF AMERICA

STATEMENT OF PURPOSE

THE GROUP FOR THE ADVANCEMENT OF PSYCHIATRY has a membership of approximately 300 psychiatrists, most of whom are organized in the form of a number of working committees. These committees direct their efforts toward the study of various aspects of psychiatry and the application of this knowledge to the fields of mental health and human relations.

Collaboration with specialists in other disciplines has been and is one of GAP's working principles. Since the formation of GAP in 1946 its members have worked closely with such other specialists as anthropologists, biologists, economists, statisticians, educators, lawyers, nurses, psychologists, sociologists, social workers, and experts in mass communication, philosophy, and semantics. GAP envisages a continuing program of work according to the following aims:

1. To collect and appraise significant data in the fields of psychiatry, mental health, and human relations;
2. To reevaluate old concepts and to develop and test new ones;
3. To apply the knowledge thus obtained for the promotion of mental health and good human relations.

GAP is an independent group, and its reports represent the composite findings and opinions of its members only, guided by its many consultants.

TEENAGE PREGNANCY: IMPACT ON ADOLESCENT DEVELOPMENT was formulated by the Committee on Adolescence. The members of this committee are listed on the next page. The following pages list the members of the other GAP committees, as well as additional membership categories and current and past officers of GAP.

Committee on Adolescence
Group for the Advancement of Psychiatry
Silvio J. Onesti, M.D., Chairman

Ian Canino, M.D.
Sherman C. Feinstein, M.D.
Warren J. Gadpaille, M.D.
Michael G. Kalogerakis, M.D.
Clarice J. Kestenbaum, M.D.
Derek Miller, M.D.

GAP Committees and Membership

COMMITTEE ON AGING
Gene D. Cohen, Rockville, Md.,
  Chairperson
Charles M. Gaitz, Houston, Tex.
Robert J. Nathan, Philadelphia, Pa.
George H. Pollock, Chicago, Ill.
Kenneth M. Sakauye, Chicago, Ill.
Charles A. Shamoian, White Plains, N.Y.
F. Conyers Thompson, Jr., Atlanta, Ga.

COMMITTEE ON CHILD PSYCHIATRY
Theodore Shapiro, New York, N.Y.,
  Chairperson
Paul L. Adams, Galveston, Tex.
James M. Bell, Canaan, N.Y.
Harlow Donald Dunton, New York, N.Y.
Joseph Fischhoff, Detroit, Mich.
Joseph M. Green, Madison, Wis.
John F. McDermott, Jr., Honolulu, Hawaii
John Schowalter, New Haven, Conn.
Peter E. Tanguay, Los Angeles, Calif.
Lenore F.C. Terr, San Francisco, Calif.

COMMITTEE ON COLLEGE STUDENTS
Kent E. Robinson, Towson, Md.,
  Chairperson
Robert L. Arnstein, Hamden, Conn.
Varda Backus, La Jolla, Calif.
Harrison P. Eddy, New York, N.Y.
Myron B. Liptzin, Chapel Hill, N.C.
Malkah Tolpin Notman, Brookline, Mass.
Gloria C. Onque, Pittsburgh, Pa.
Elizabeth Aub Reid, Cambridge, Mass.
Earle Silber, Chevy Chase, Md.
Tom G. Stauffer, White Plains, N.Y.

COMMITTEE ON CULTURAL PSYCHIATRY
Ezra E.H. Griffith, New Haven, Conn.,
  Chairperson
Edward F. Foulks, Philadelphia, Pa.
Pedro Ruiz, Houston, Tex.
John P. Spiegel, Waltham, Mass.
Ronald M. Wintrob, Providence, R.I.
Joe Yamamoto, Los Angeles, Calif.

COMMITTEE ON THE FAMILY
W. Robert Beavers, Dallas, Tex.,
  Chairperson
Ellen M. Berman, Merrion, Pa.
Lee Combrinck-Graham, Philadelphia, Pa.

Ira D. Glick, New York, N.Y.
Frederick Gottlieb, Los Angeles, Calif.
Henry U. Grunebaum, Cambridge, Mass.
Herta A. Guttman, Montreal, Quebec
Judith Landau-Stanton, Rochester, N.Y.
Ann L. Price, Hartford, Conn.

COMMITTEE ON GOVERNMENTAL AGENCIES
William W. Van Stone, Palo Alto, Calif.,
  Chairperson
James P. Cattell, San Diego, Calif.
Sidney S. Goldensohn, New York, N.Y.
Naomi Heller, Washington, D.C.
Roger Peele, Washington, D.C.

COMMITTEE ON HANDICAPS
Norman R. Bernstein, Chicago, Ill.,
  Chairperson
Meyer S. Gunther, Chicago, Ill.
William H. Sack, Portland, Oreg.
William A. Sonis, Minneapolis, Minn.
George Tarjan, Los Angeles, Calif.
Thomas G. Webster, Washington, D.C.
Henry H. Work, Bethesda, Md.

COMMITTEE ON INTERNATIONAL RELATIONS
Francis F. Barnes, Chevy Chase, Md.,
  Chairperson
Robert M. Dorn, Sacramento, Calif.
John S. Kafka, Washington, D.C.
Edward Khantzian, Haverhill, Mass.
John E. Mack, Chestnut Hill, Mass.
Rita R. Rogers, Palos Verdes Estates, Calif.
Bertram H. Schaffner, New York, N.Y.
Stephen B. Shanfield, Tucson, Ariz.
Vamik D. Volkan, Charlottesville, Va.

COMMITTEE ON MEDICAL EDUCATION
David R. Hawkins, Chicago, Ill.,
  Chairperson
Gene Abroms, Ardmore, Pa.
Charles M. Culver, Hanover, N.H.
Steven L. Dubovsky, Denver, Colo.
Saul I. Harrison, Torrance, Calif.
Harold I. Lief, Philadelphia, Pa.
Carol Nadelson, Boston, Mass.
Carolyn B. Robinowitz, Washington, D.C.
Stephen C. Scheiber, Tucson, Ariz.
Veva H. Zimmerman, New York, N.Y.

COMMITTEE ON MENTAL HEALTH SERVICES
George F. Wilson, Belle Mead, N.J.,
 Chairperson
Allan Beigel, Tucson, Ariz.
Merrill T. Eaton, Omaha, Nebr.
John M. Hamilton, Baltimore, Md.
W. Walter Menninger, Topeka, Kans.
Jose Maria Santiago, Tucson, Ariz.
Herzl R. Spiro, Milwaukee, Wis.
William L. Webb, Jr., Hartford, Conn.
Jack A. Wolford, Pittsburgh, Pa.

COMMITTEE ON PREVENTIVE PSYCHIATRY
Stephen Fleck, New Haven, Conn.,
 Chairperson
Viola W. Bernard, New York, N.Y.
Stanley I. Greenspan, Bethesda, Md.
William H. Hetznecker, Philadelphia, Pa.
Richard, G. Morrill, Boston, Mass.
Harris B. Peck, New Rochelle, N.Y.
Anne Marie Wolf, Philadelphia, Pa.

COMMITTEE ON PSYCHIATRY AND
 THE COMMUNITY
John A. Talbott, New York, N.Y.
 Chairperson
C. Knight Aldrich, Charlottesville, Va.
H. Richard Lamb, Los Angeles, Calif.
Kenneth Minkoff, Somerville, Mass.
John C. Nemiah, Hanover, N.H.
Rebecca L. Potter, Tucson, Ariz.
Alexander S. Rogawski, Los Angeles, Calif.
John J. Schwab, Louisville, Ky.
Charles B. Wilkinson, Kansas City, Mo.

COMMITTEE ON PSYCHIATRY AND LAW
Jonas R. Rappeport, Baltimore, Md.,
 Chairperson
Park E. Dietz, Charlottesville, Va.
John Donnelly, Hartford, Conn.
Carl P. Malmquist, Minneapolis, Minn.
Herbert C. Modlin, Topeka, Kans.
Phillip J. Resnick, Cleveland, Ohio
Loren J. Roth, Pittsburgh, Pa.
Joseph Satten, San Francisco, Calif.
William D. Weitzel, Lexington, Ky.
Howard V. Zonana, New Haven, Conn.

COMMITTEE ON PSYCHIATRY AND RELIGION
Albert J. Lubin, Woodside, Calif.,
 Chairperson

Sidney Furst, Bronx, N.Y.
Richard C. Lewis, New Haven, Conn.
Earl A. Loomis, Jr., Augusta, Ga.
Mortimer Ostow, Bronx, N.Y.
Sally K. Severino, White Plains, N.Y.
Clyde R. Snyder, PSF, Calif.
Michael R. Zales, Greenwich, Conn.

COMMITTEE ON PSYCHIATRY IN INDUSTRY
Barrie S. Greiff, Cambridge, Mass.,
 Chairperson
Peter L. Brill, Philadelphia, Pa.
Duane Q. Hagen, St. Louis, Mo.
R. Edward Huffman, Asheville, N.C.
David E. Morrison, Palatine, Ill.
David B. Robbins, Chappaqua, N.Y.
Jay B. Rohrlich, New York, N.Y.
Clarence J. Rowe, St. Paul, Minn.
Jeffrey L. Speller, Alexandria, Va.
John Wakefield, Saratoga, Calif.

COMMITTEE ON PSYCHOPATHOLOGY
David A. Adler, Boston, Mass.,
 Chairperson
Jeffrey Berlant, San Anselmo, Calif.
Doyle I. Carson, Dallas, Tex.
Robert E. Drake, Hanover, N.H.
Howard H. Goldman, Rockville, Md.
Johanna A. Hoffman, Richmond, Va.
Richard E. Renneker, Los Angeles, Calif.

COMMITTEE ON PUBLIC EDUCATION
Robert A. Solow, Beverly Hills, Calif.,
 Chairperson
Susan J. Blumenthal, Rockville, Md.
Robert J. Campbell, New York, N.Y.
Keith H. Johansen, Dallas, Tex.
Steven E. Katz, New York, N.Y.
Norman L. Loux, Sellersville, Pa.
Harvey L. Ruben, New Haven, Conn.
Kenneth N. Vogtsberger, San Antonio, Tex.

COMMITTEE ON RESEARCH
Robert Cancro, New York, N.Y.,
 Chairperson
Kenneth Z. Altshuler, Dallas, Tex.
Jack A. Grebb, New York, N.Y.
John H. Greist, Madison, Wisc.
Jerry M. Lewis, Dallas, Tex.

GAP Committees and Membership

Morris A. Lipton, Chapel Hill, N.C.
John G. Looney, Dallas, Tex.
Zebulon Taintor, Orangeburg, N.Y.

COMMITTEE ON SOCIAL ISSUES
Ian E. Alger, New York, N.Y.,
 Chairperson
William R. Beardslee, Boston, Mass.
Paul J. Fink, Philadelphia, Pa.
Henry J. Gault, Highland Park, Ill.
Judith H. Gold, Halifax, Nova Scotia
Roderic Gorney, Los Angeles, Calif.
Martha J. Kirkpatrick, Los Angeles, Calif.
Perry Ottenberg, Philadelphia, Pa.
Kendon W. Smith, Piermont, N.Y.

COMMITTEE ON THERAPEUTIC CARE
Milton Kramer, Cincinnati, Ohio,
 Chairperson
Bernard Bandler, Cambridge, Mass.
Thomas E. Curtis, Chapel Hill, N.C.
Robert W. Gibson, Towson, Md.
Donald W. Hammersley, Washington, D.C.
William B. Hunter, III, Albuquerque, N.M.
Roberto L. Jimenez, San Antonio, Tex.
Melvin Sabshin, Washington, D.C.

COMMITTEE ON THERAPY
Allan D. Rosenblatt, La Jolla, Calif.,
 Chairperson
Henry W. Brosin, Tucson, Ariz.
Eugene B. Feigelson, Brooklyn, N.Y.
Robert Michels, New York, N.Y.
Andrew P. Morrison, Cambridge, Mass.
William C. Offenkrantz, Milwaukee, Wis.

CONTRIBUTING MEMBERS
John E. Adams, Gainesville, Fl.
Carlos C. Alden, Jr., Buffalo, N.Y.

Mary Ann B. Bartusis, Morrisville, Pa.
Eric A. Baum, Akron, Ohio
Spencer Bayles, Houston, Tex.
Aaron T. Beck, Wynnewood, Pa.
C. Christian Beels, New York, N.Y.
Elissa P. Benedek, Ann Arbor, Mich.
Sidney Berman, Washington, D.C.
Wilfred Bloomberg, Cambridge, Mass.
H. Keith H. Brodie, Durham, N.C.
Charles M. Bryant, San Francisco, Calif.

Ewald W. Busse, Durham, N.C.
Robert N. Butler, New York, N.Y.

Eugene M. Caffey, Jr., Bowie, Md.
Paul Chodoff, Washington, D.C.
Ian L.W. Clancey, Ontario, Canada
Sanford I. Cohen, Boston, Mass.

James S. Eaton, Jr., Washington, D.C.
Lloyd C. Elam, Nashville, Tenn.
Stanley H. Eldred, Belmont, Mass.
Joseph T. English, New York, N.Y.
Louis C. English, Pomona, N.Y.

Archie R. Foley, New York, N.Y.
Daniel X. Freedman, Chicago, Ill.

Alexander Gralnick, Port Chester, N.Y.
Milton Greenblatt, Sepulveda, Calif.
Lawrence F. Greenleigh, Los Angeles, Calif.
Ernest M. Gruenberg, Bethesda, Md.
Jon E. Gudeman, Lexington, Mass.

Seymour L. Halleck, Chapel Hill, N.C.
Stanley Hammons, Lexington, Ky.
J. Cotter Hirschberg, Topeka, Kans.

Jay Katz, New Haven, Conn.
James A. Knight, New Orleans, La.
Othilda M. Krug, Cincinnati, Ohio

Alan I. Levenson, Tucson, Ariz.
Ruth W. Lidz, Woodbridge, Conn.
Orlando B. Lightfoot, Boston, Mass.
Reginald S. Lourie, Chevy Chase, Md.

John A. MacLeod, Cincinnati, Ohio
Leo Madow, Philadelphia, Pa.
Charles A. Malone, Cleveland, Ohio
Sidney G. Margolin, Denver, Colo.
Peter A. Martin, Bloomfield Hills, Mich.
Ake Mattsson, New York, N.Y.
Alan A. McLean, Westport, Conn.
David Mendell, Houston, Tex.
Roy W. Menninger, Topeka, Kans.
Mary E. Mercer, Nyack, N.Y.

Joseph D. Noshpitz, Washington, D.C.
Charles P. O'Brien, Philadelphia, Pa.
Bernard L. Pacella, New York, N.Y.
Herbert Pardes, New York, N.Y.

Norman L. Paul, Lexington, Mass.
Marvin E. Perkins, Salem, Va.
Betty J. Pfefferbaum, Houston, Tex.
Charles A. Pinderhughes, Bedford, Mass.

David N. Ratnavale, Bethesda, Md.
W. Donald Ross, Cincinnati, Ohio
Lester H. Rudy, Chicago, Ill.
George E. Ruff, Philadelphia, Pa.

David S. Sanders, Los Angeles, Calif.
Donald J. Scherl, Brooklyn, N.Y.
Kurt O. Schlesinger, San Francisco, Calif.
Charles Shagass, Philadelphia, Pa.
Miles F. Shore, Boston, Mass.
Albert J. Silverman, Ann Arbor, Mich.
Benson R. Snyder, Cambridge, Mass.
David A. Soskis, Bala Cynwyd, Pa.
Jeanne Spurlock, Washington, D.C.
Brandt F. Steele, Denver, Colo.
Rutherford B. Stevens, New York, N.Y.
Alan A. Stone, Cambridge, Mass.
Robert E. Switzer, Dunn Loring, Va.

Perry C. Talkington, Dallas, Tex.
Bryce Templeton, Philadelphia, Pa.
Prescott W. Thompson, Beaverton, Oreg.
Joe P. Tupin, Sacramento, Calif.
John A. Turner, San Francisco, Calif.

Warren T. Vaughan, Jr., Portola Valley, Calif.

Robert S. Wallerstein, San Francisco, Calif.
Andrew S. Watson, Ann Arbor, Mich.
Bryant M. Wedge, Washington, D.C.
Joseph B. Wheelwright, Kentfield, Calif.
Robert L. Williams, Houston, Tex.
Paul Tyler Wilson, Bethesda, Md.
Sherwyn M. Woods, Los Angeles, Calif.

Kent A. Zimmerman, Berkeley, Calif.
Israel Zwerling, Philadelphia, Pa.

LIFE MEMBERS
C. Knight Aldrich, Charlottesville, Va.
Bernard Bandler, Cambridge, Mass.
Walter E. Barton, Hartland, Vt.
Ivan C. Berlien, Coral Gables, Fla.
Viola W. Bernard, New York, N.Y.
Murray Bowen, Chevy Chase, Md.

Henry W. Brosin, Tucson, Ariz.
John Donnelly, Hartford, Conn.
O. Spurgeon English, Narberth, Pa.
Dana L. Farnsworth, Boston, Mass.
Stephen Fleck, New Haven, Conn.
Jerome Frank, Baltimore, Md.
Robert S. Garber, Osprey, Fl.
Paul E. Huston, Iowa City, Iowa
Margaret M. Lawrence, Pomona, N.Y.
Harold I. Lief, Philadelphia, Pa.
Judd Marmor, Los Angeles, Calif.
Karl A. Menninger, Topeka, Kans.
Herbert C. Modlin, Topeka, Kans.
John C. Nemiah, Hanover, N.H.
Mabel Ross, Sun City, Ariz.
Julius Schreiber, Washington, D.C.
George Tarjan, Los Angeles, Calif.
Jack A. Wolford, Pittsburgh, Pa.
Henry H. Work, Bethesda, Md.

BOARD OF DIRECTORS

OFFICERS

President
Michael R. Zales
Edgewood Drive
Greenwich, Conn. 06830

President-Elect
Jerry M. Lewis
Timberlawn Hospital
P.O. Box 270789
Dallas, Tex. 75227

Secretary
Allan Beigel
30 Camino Español
Tucson, Ariz. 85716

Treasurer
Charles B. Wilkinson
600 E. 22nd Street
Kansas City, Mo. 64108

Board Members

Merrill T. Eaton
Carol Nadelson
Roger Peele
John J. Schwab

GAP Committees and Membership

Past Presidents

*William C. Menninger	1946-51
Jack R. Ewalt	1951-53
Walter E. Barton	1953-55
*Sol W. Ginsburg	1955-57
Dana L. Farnsworth	1957-59
*Marion E. Kenworthy	1959-61
Henry W. Brosin	1961-63
*Leo H. Bartemeier	1963-65
Robert S. Garber	1965-67
Herbert C. Modlin	1967-69
John Donnelly	1969-71
George Tarjan	1971-73
Judd Marmor	1973-75
John C. Nemiah	1975-77
Jack A. Wolford	1977-79
Robert W. Gibson	1979-81
*Jack Weinberg	1981-82
Henry H. Work	1982-85

PUBLICATIONS BOARD

Chairman
John C. Nemiah
4 Rayton Rd.
Hanover, N.H. 03755

Robert L. Arnstein
Stanley I. Greenspan
Milton Kramer
W. Walter Menninger
Alexander S. Rogawski
Robert A. Solow

Consultant
Merrill T. Eaton

Ex-Officio
Michael R. Zales
Jerry M. Lewis

CONTRIBUTORS
Abbott Laboratories
American Charitable Fund
Mrs. Morris Aron
Dr. and Mrs. Richard Aron
Maurice Falk Medical Fund
Mrs. Carol Gold
Grove Foundation, Inc.
Miss Gayle Groves
Ittleson Foundation, Inc.
Mrs. Allan H. Kalmus
Marion E. Kenworthy—Sarah H. Swift
  Foundation, Inc.
McNeil Pharmaceutical
Phillips Foundation
Sandoz, Inc.
Smith Kline Beckman Corporation
Tappanz Foundation, Inc.
The Upjohn Company
van Amerigen Foundation, Inc.
Wyeth Laboratories

———

*deceased

COMMITTEE ACKNOWLEDGMENTS

This report is written for all those who work with adolescents, for those who are involved with various aspects of their lives, and for those who wish to understand their world.

The Committee dedicates this report to the late Maurice R. Friend, M.D., one of its members, whose enthusiasm, ideas, and wisdom were an inspiration to us all.

Warren J. Gadpaille, M.D., served as chairman of the Committee during the initial stage of this report.

Harrison P. Eddy, M.D., was a member of the Committee throughout the preparation of this report.

Over the course of the report three Sol W. Ginsburg Fellows, M. Gillian McLintock, M.D., Alan Brown, M.D., and Pamela A. Felder, M.D., made valuable contributions to its formulation and content.

We are indebted to W. Godrey Cobliner, Ph.D., and Lorraine Klerman, Dr.P.H., for their thoughtful reading of our report in its final stages and their helpful suggestions.

The Committee thanks Jean Galligan Pallone for her invaluable secretarial and library assistance and Barbara Panza for her skilled use of the word processor.

CONTENTS

Statement of Purpose v
GAP Committees and Membership vii
Committee Acknowledgments xiii
Introduction xvii

1. Dimensions of the Problem 3
2. Adolescent Development and Sexuality 7
3. Context and Meaning of Pregnancy: Teenage Mothers 15
4. Context and Meaning of Pregnancy: Fathers 25
5. Psychological and Developmental Consequences of Teenage Pregnancy and Parenthood 33
6. Health and Socioeconomic Consequences of Teenage Pregnancy and Parenthood 43
7. Interventions and Recommendations 57
8. Summary and Conclusions 69

Appendix: Programs for High-Risk Adolescent Mothers and Their Infants 71
Index 77

INTRODUCTION

Books about adolescents usually are written by adults. This one is no exception. It is the product of discussions by a group of child and adolescent psychiatrists concerned about crises among adolescents in our society and the effects of these crises on adolescent growth and development. We view crises as destabilizing events that may have short- or long-term disruptive consequences.

Adolescents often trouble adults. Their behavior distresses them; their future worries them. Adults need strong individuals to join them one day as co-workers and colleagues who can assist them, support them, and eventually replace them. Adults provide for the security, welfare, education, and training of the young. They await fulfillment of adolescent promise; delay and deviation evoke their dismay.

Adolescents possess the capacity to engage in adult activities. They are physically strong and sexually fertile. At their best they are able to grasp and employ abstract ideas, solve intellectual problems, and invent methods and concepts. Curiosity about their past, exploration of their present, and concern for their future compel adolescents to assess society and the adults who have established it for them. When their challenge leads to adult reexamination and change of practice and values, adolescents modify the world they are about to enter.

Adolescents have potential, but they lack the knowledge, experience, and judgment attained through discharge of adult responsibilities. Adolescents need adult support, but many reject adult guidance. Too often such guidance echoes sounds heard in childhood; ultimately, necessity and trial validate or refute its worth. Adolescents face tasks of transition; the future depends on their meeting these tasks successfully.

In the recent past many adolescents opposed and rebuked the adult world. They reviled an unpopular war, repudiated materialistic pursuits, and rejected parental life-styles. At present, most adolescents do not appear to question adult values so severely. They want what adults have; they want to do what adults do. Security-minded, industrious adolescents study and work toward eventual power and position. Other adolescents insist on immediate possession and gratification; they grasp at adult attractions and obey the urges of their bodies.

Adolescence, even under the best of circumstances, is a stressful phase of life. Young people face the impact of puberty, expanding physical and psychosocial powers, and emergence from family into a seemingly foreign society. Adolescents must begin to acquire the skills and discipline of apprenticeship and the ability to study, work, play, and express curiosity through social exploration if they are to transform the immaturity, habits, and attitudes of childhood into responsible adult functions.

Adolescents may, on the basis of immaturity alone, indulge in actions that can result in disruptive consequences. Nevertheless, most adolescents negotiate this difficult period without seriously harmful behavior. The ability to do so requires adequate developmental preparations, contributed to by appropriate biological, cognitive, emotional, familial, and societal influences. Conditions that compromise the developmental preparation for adolescence render the individual at far greater risk for a range of behaviors that constitute crises with potentially damaging consequences.

Compromised development can be further impaired by passive retreat or impulsive acts. These can include school failure or withdrawal, attempted suicide, criminal assault, violence, theft, fire setting, running away, vagrancy, drug abuse, prostitution, and illegitimate pregnancy. The effects

Introduction

of such behaviors are not limited to their immediate consequences. Disruptive actions of great magnitude lead to crises in development, crises that threaten to abbreviate, distort, or interrupt the developmental process of adolescence itself.

Human development, from infancy through old age, necessitates a series of increasingly complex tasks. Strengths and supports wax and wane. Although crises provide opportunities for successful mastery, they may become obstacles unremoved, barriers unsurmounted, or forces leading to disorganization. Adolescent crises often become societal problems. Each crisis compels adult society to respond. Each crisis affords society an opportunity to evolve and accommodate inner growth, but, as with the individual, each crisis may provoke social disruption. Crises that interfere with adolescent development threaten society as a whole.

We have chosen as the topic for this report the problem of pregnancy during adolescence. Pregnancy at any age engenders developmental change; in the immature, it creates developmental crisis. Pregnancy during adolescence thus compounds the stresses of two normative developmental stages and endangers the successful resolution of either one. Childbirth and parenthood add tasks, choices, and responsibilities. Developmental failures in parents place their children at biological, psychological, and social risk. Among crises during adolescence, pregnancy endangers not only the individual and society, but also the unborn child.

As psychiatrists, we accept the task to foster human development. We are called upon to relieve suffering that results from developmental deviation, disruption, or arrest. We assess risks and benefits of competing choices of intervention. We are aware that personal belief, professional conviction, religious faith, cultural practice, and societal injunction all influence decision and outcome. We believe that professionals and individuals in society should be informed of what is known of human development and its disorder, the various means of intervention to prevent or diminish disorder, and the consequences of choosing each alternative.

The crisis of teenage pregnancy provides us with an exemplary opportunity to propose our views. It is our hope that ideas generated by the considerations here presented will find application in this and other matters of equal importance.

CRISES OF ADOLESCENCE

Teenage Pregnancy: Impact on Adolescent Development

1
DIMENSIONS OF THE PROBLEM

Teenage pregnancy is a major biological, mental health, and social problem. The Alan Guttmacher Institute (1981), in reviewing studies involving thousands of teenagers, called the situation "epidemic." Far more teenagers are becoming sexually active than has been reported in past generations. Twenty percent of adolescents 14 years of age or younger are reported to be active sexually. The rate of increase is most dramatic among white adolescent girls, whose sexual activity has doubled during the past five years. These teenagers are increasingly from the nonminority middle class, as well as from the traditionally sexually active lower socioeconomic groups.

Each year more than one million adolescents aged 15 to 19 in the United States become pregnant. Two-thirds of these pregnancies are conceived out of wedlock, and one-fifth of all births in the United States are to women still in their teens. While in earlier generations unwed adolescent mothers, especially those from middle and upper socioeconomic groups, often gave their babies up for adoption, now many keep their babies. In one study as many as 95 percent kept their babies. The problem was not only of teenage pregnancy, but also of teenage baby keeping and deficient motherhood (Fisher & Scharf, 1980).

The younger a woman was when she first gave birth, the more likely it was that she came from a family of poverty. One-third of early adolescent mothers were from below the federal poverty line. Those who first gave birth during mid-adolescence were twice as likely to be poor, and even late-adolescent mothers were 1.4 times more likely to be poor compared to adult mothers. Teenage mothers were less likely to work and more likely to be on welfare. After giving birth, most of the mothers had neither full- nor part-time employment. Clearly, many pregnant teenagers are poorly nourished, do not receive early and adequate care, are likely to be victims of environmental deprivation and poor housing with its concomitant problems, and may be subjected to additional risks through the abuse of drugs and alcohol.

Jane was 14 years old and seven months pregnant when she was evaluated by the social worker in a center for adolescent pregnancy. She lived with her mother, her 18-year-old drug-abusing brother, her 16-year-old unmarried sister, that sister's two-year-old son, and a 10-year-old sister. Her alcoholic and wife-abusing father had abandoned the family nearly 10 years earlier, but memories of his drunken fights with her mother still troubled Jane. Her mother was totally dependent on her welfare check.

Jane's early life had been traumatic and emotionally deprived. Her mother seemed exhausted and unable to cope. Jane was frequently left with different neighbors for days on end. When no adult was available, Jane was left in the care of her slightly older sister and brother. By the time she entered school, she was considered overactive and undisciplined. Her concentration and her persistence in learning tasks was poor, and school was fraught with frustration and failure. Guidance counselors were unable to engage her mother's cooperation, and by sixth grade, although Jane was considered intelligent, she was two years behind in math and reading. She had a few friends, but her opportunities to develop social skills were curtailed by her mother's constant need for help at home.

Jane was 12 years old when she met 13-year-old Lawrence at school. He, too, had an alcoholic father, a depleted mother, and a brother high on drugs. The two "fell in love" and became inseparable. Neither had had prior sexual experience, and both were ignorant of birth control methods. Jane became pregnant soon after menarche.

Adolescent girls, for a variety of reasons, are at higher risk for complications of pregnancy, abortion, or childbearing than are women in their twenties and early thirties. The risk is higher for their infants as well; fetal and neonatal morbidity and mortality are more frequent. In addition to the biological problems of adolescent pregnancy and childbirth, social and psychological factors further limit the emotional, physical, and intellectual development of mother and child.

These observations, however, do not provide a complete picture. Teenage pregnancy does not constitute a syndrome, and teenage mothers are not a homogeneous group. There are considerable differences in the psychological meaning of pregnancy for each individual girl regardless of her social class, and there are class and culture differences in outcome patterns of adolescent pregnancy. Pregnancy, particularly for midadolescents, need not be hazardous. In some nonindustrial societies, childbirth typically begins only a few years after puberty. Customary support systems, such as extended families and social networks, may serve to provide opportunities for learning mothering through communal task sharing and modeling.

The complexity of modern industrial technological culture makes the positive outcome of adolescent pregnancy far less likely. In the context of the cultural demand for advanced education and specialized skills, early pregnancy compromises development. For many, this leads to an interruption of school, work goals, and career plans. For most, it interferes with successful completion of the process of adolescence.

REFERENCES

Fisher, S.M., & Scharf, K.R. Teenage pregnancy: An anthropological, sociological, and pschological overview. *Adolescent Psychiatry*, 8:393–403, 1980.

Alan Guttmacher Institute. *Teenage pregnancy: The problem that hasn't gone away.* New York, 1981.

2
ADOLESCENT DEVELOPMENT AND SEXUALITY

Adolescence is a developmental stage that bridges childhood dependency and adult autonomy. It is the stage during which adult reproductive sexuality is born and matures. Consequently, the tasks that confront adolescents as they progress through the teen years are inextricably bound to their unfolding sexuality.

Adolescents are faced with the need to loosen their parental ties. Children and adolescents, who have been nurtured and provided for by family and society, must eventually learn to function as independent adults. Relative autonomy from undue parental influence prepares the way for optimal functioning as future parents in families of their own making. Toward this end adolescents complete their gender identity. Although gender identity is primarily established within the earliest years of life, it is in adolescence that acceptance of one's own body and sexual role must occur before the choice of a desired sexual partner can be made. Gilligan (1982), from her studies of preadolescent and adolescent girls, has emphasized the importance of the nature and meaning of relationships to the process of identity formation. Adolescents form new emotional bonds. While maintaining love for their parents and siblings, adolescents shift their emotional focus toward other adults and peers, eventually seeking sexual partners, intimacy, and responsibility in love relationships.

Adolescent cognitive development progressively permits

more mature contemplation. Adolescents develop the ability to consider possibilities; they can explore potential consequences without having to commit thought to action and experience the results; they can plan a future. Realistic self-assessment and appropriate goals for future work replace unrealistic expectations. Moral values and belief systems strengthen during this period although challenged on many fronts. With success, the completion of these tasks leads to the formation of a stable adolescent and adult identity.

These tasks of adolescence are not easily accomplished given the timing of the biological, psychodynamic, psychosocial, and cognitive development of the adolescent. Biological puberty heralds the onset of adolescence, six months to two years earlier in girls than in boys. Physiological and anatomical changes continue well into the middle or late teens. New sensations, drives, and capabilities require considerable time to be integrated and consolidated into the adolescent's sense of self.

In both sexes genital stimulation can be recognized at an early age. Masturbation occurs in infants and children as a normal means of pleasure and self-solace. In adolescence masturbation provides a way of expressing and managing powerful sexual urges. It can be viewed as a method of experimenting with one's own physiological and psychological capacities.

The midadolescent girl is in a vulnerable position regarding her self-concept and societal roles and will often experience difficulty coping with her rapid physical changes. Her attitude toward menarche and sex in general is often influenced by her mother's attitude. If the mother's feminine self-image is unsatisfactory, she may convey negative feelings about female attributes and female bodies.

Masturbation is a central issue in the development of girls and boys. Girls can frequently deny that the pleasurable sensation derived from pressure on the inner thigh is a masturbatory act, but boys, with their obvious erections, cannot.

Adolescent Development and Sexuality 9

Guilt feelings, in relation to moral behavior and incestuous fantasies, can act as powerful deterrents to otherwise natural urges.

For boys and girls masturbation may become a significant developmental activity at puberty and a method whereby the experience of sexual excitement is allied with fantasies about sexual involvement. Pubertal masturbation is a way station on the road to adult sexuality.

Through masturbation a boy, particularly, may learn to master a seemingly uncontrollable body. Erections are more frequent as puberty proceeds and arouse awareness of the feeling that a part of the body is, and his feelings are, out of control. The masturbatory act helps to control tumescence and detumescence. In addition, through masturbation the boy can learn to separate aggressive and sexual impulses; a primitive mixture of aggression and sexual fantasies can become clarified and reworked.

In middle-class culture, masturbation continues usually into adulthood by which time occasional intercourse or periods of regular sexual involvement with another person have become the preferable activity. The sexuality of adolescents is initially more experimental than loving. Heterosexual exploration in midadolescence has less the function of establishing an intimate tie than of helping to explore and understand new sensations (Kestenbaum, 1979). It may also be conducted in response to peer pressure and from a sense of competition. It is a major problem that more adolescents are beginning sexual intercourse prematurely.

> Susan was a 14-year-old honor student from a "liberated" home. Her mother assumed that she was a responsible girl, gave her a talk about "the facts of life" after her first menstrual period, and told her she could now handle her own private life. But one effect on Susan of her parents' permissive attitude had been that they had not helped her to learn which qualities in herself she could be proud of and which were less admirable. Without an internalized sense of self-esteem, Su-

san was determined to be popular at all costs. At an unchaperoned party one night, she engaged in intercourse with a boy who was apparently interested only in conquest. She was subsequently humiliated and ashamed and was later found to be pregnant.

The capacity to delay immediate gratification in favor of greater future gain is a mark of maturity. The younger the adolescent, the more it may be appropriate, even developmentally necessary, for the adolescent to postpone some kinds of sexual gratification. Coitus may be something for which many adolescents are not yet ready. For mature adolescents, responsible sexual activity may be appropriate.

According to studies by Chilman (1978), premarital intercourse rates in a 10-year span from 1965 to 1975 increased 50 percent for white males and 300 percent for white females. By the 1970s, first intercourse had occurred at an earlier age than in prior studies. One-fourth of white males and females had experienced coitus by age 16, while by the same age over 90 percent of black males and about 50 percent of black females were sexually active. Kantner and Zelnik (1972) found that by age 19, 47 percent of females in a large probability sample had had intercourse. Five years later, the same researchers found comparable figures to be substantially increased as the adolescents tended to have more partners and more frequent intercourse (Zelnik & Kantner, 1977). More recently, Bell and Coughey (1980) reported that 65 percent of college women aged 19 or younger had had intercourse, and some studies found nonvirgin and frequency of intercourse rates higher among girls than boys at the high-school level (Jessor & Jessor, 1975).

It seems to us that healthy, responsible adolescent sexuality (whether or not involving intercourse) derives from experiences in families that foster personal and sexual maturity. Within such families, members are encouraged to feel and teach love for one another and concern for each other's well-being, to foster interest in many kinds of knowledge, to respect one another, to adhere to stated values, to pursue stage-appropriate emotional independence and development of autonomous thought and decision making, to consider sexual activity with respect to rights and responsibilities, to expect responsible behavior in return for privileges and freedoms, and to recognize the rights of all to develop and mature in individual ways and at individual paces.

The psychological significance of pregnancy has its own impact on the psychological development and sexuality of adolescent girls and boys. Although adolescent boys often are deeply involved with the meaning of pregnancy and with the mother-to-be, pregnancy must have a far greater meaning for the girl. She is the one who must carry the fetus in her body and usually is the one who must provide nurture and primary care for years thereafter. Fantasies about pregnancy, of course, begin before puberty, but only those reflective of adolescent development will be touched upon here.

For a girl, having ideas of a fetus being part of herself, of her own nourishment, and inseparable as a distinct being may blur her own boundaries; having a baby to nourish and nurture may be like nourishing her still-infantile self or being nurtured again by her own mother. In this way she may express the need to remain mother's cared-for and dependent child. At the same time, the baby may be considered as competing for mother's nurture as a sibling, arousing jealousy and rage. A baby may be a precious gift for mother or a bodily product to be withheld in defiance. The baby, as something mother cannot force her to give up, may be valued as proof of autonomy; the baby may be devalued and rejected if associated with disgusting products of elimination.

Such fantasies may occur in young healthy girls from emotionally healthy families. They diminish in intensity as girls separate from their childhood-dependent relationship with their parents, integrate their sexuality into a mature body image and sexual identity, and focus their drives on appropriate heterosexual objects and actions. If there is interference with the resolution of such concepts, they may be acted out through premature pregnancy and may lead to harmful interactions between the girl, the baby, her parents, and the father.

Pregnancy is associated with independence, power, and adult status. Teenage girls often fantasize pregnancy as a way to break away from parental dependence, a way to be mother's equal. A girl may also imagine that pregnancy can accomplish this through attracting or entrapping a boy who will liberate her from her family. Pregnancy, used in these ways, signals incomplete or failed development, and its consequences impair development even more.

There are also inappropriate fears in teenage girls associated with pregnancy and childbirth that are gradually resolved in the process of a healthy adolescence. Misconceptions associated with the impregnation or delivery may be holdovers from childhood, such as fears of excessive injury or damage. In some cultures children grow up observing pregnant mothers and sisters and watching deliveries. In other cultures, such as in parts of our own in which children are typically shielded from reproductive realities, unrealistic fantasies may persist more strongly into adolescence. Gradual, nontraumatic, adolescent sexual experimentation, plus information and the cognitive maturation to integrate it, eventually replaces such fantasies with reality. To the extent that misconceptions and unrealistic wishes persist, some therapeutic intervention may be helpful.

Teenage boys are not immune from analogous fantasies about pregnancy, childbirth, and infants. They, too, identify with infants in positive or envious and rivalrous ways. They may equate impregnating a girl with winning out over other males, though rivalry often involves only the ability to have sexual intercourse and to satisfy a woman. Many boys equate manhood with fathering a child; this leads to using girls for self-affirming purposes. Boys as well as girls may have fearsome fantasies about fetuses and about damage to mothers.

When pregnancy and parenthood come after the tasks of adolescence have been completed, after the fantasies of childhood have been appropriately resolved, they foster development. For women and for men, pregnancy and childbirth can provide biological fulfillment, identification with the parent of the same sex, and affirmation of sexual identity. Parenthood brings responsibilities for a new generation, benefits from child-rearing pleasures, and opportunities for continued development.

REFERENCES

Bell, R.R., & Coughey, K. Premarital sexual experience among college females, 1958, 1968 and 1978. *Family Relations*, 29:353–357, 1980.

Chilman, C.S. *Adolescent sexuality in a changing American society*. Washington, DC: US Government Printing Office, 1978.

Gilligan, C. *In a different voice*. Cambridge, MA: Harvard University Press, 1982.

Jessor, S.L., & Jessor, R. Transition from virginity to nonvirginity among youth: A social-psychological study over time. *Developmental Psychology*, 11:473–484, 1975.

Kantner, J.F., & Zelnik, M. Sexual experiences of young unmarried women in the U.S. *Family Planning Perspectives*, 4:9–17, 1972.

Kestenbaum, C.J. Current sexual attitudes, societal pressures, and the middle-class adolescent girl. *Adolescent Psychiatry*, 7:147–156, 1979.

Zelnik, M., & Kantner, J.F. Sexual and contraceptive experiences of young unmarried women in the United States, 1976 and 1971. *Family Planning Perspectives*, 9:55–71, 1977.

3
CONTEXT AND MEANING OF PREGNANCY: TEENAGE MOTHERS

Sociocultural factors are major determinants of values, belief systems, attitudes toward oneself and others, personal and career goals, and motivations for growth and progress. The demoralizing effects on adolescents are enormous in such conditions as social disorganization, poverty, poor and crowded housing, inadequate human services, and family disintegration. These factors make parents unavailable physically and emotionally to supervise children who are thrust into a world of frightening and primitive street values.

One way to conceptualize the factors conducive to teenage pregnancy is to separate them into psychological and sociocultural influences. It is immediately obvious that these categories are not mutually exclusive. The socioeconomic milieu strongly influences psychological development and emotional attitudes. There are patterns of adolescent sexual behavior and of pregnancy that are influenced by the socioeconomic environment.

Many families feel locked into a life of continuing deprivation with little to look forward to in terms of higher education, rewarding jobs, happy marriages, and adequate income. Teenagers in such families may see little benefit in deferring gratification and planning for the future. Rubin (1976) found adolescent premarital intercourse followed by early marriage to be common. Often the marriage took place to legitimate a pregnancy.

The majority of urban adolescents become heterosexually active before marriage (Furstenberg, 1976; Kantner & Zelnik, 1972). Their life situations, their needs for self-expression, their desires to be "real men" or "real women," and the socioeconomic forces within their environments are conducive to sexual behavior. There seem few other ways to gain a sense of self-expression and status. Jobs are in short supply and low in both pay and status. It is estimated that youth unemployment in urban ghettos is over 50 percent. Schools are often of poor quality, and the education offered may have little demonstrable return in terms of present or future employment.

Socioeconomic deprivation places burdens on families and adolescents that increase the statistical risk of pregnancy. However, in the midst of the most crushing poverty and social disintegration there are fertile teenage girls who do not become pregnant. There are sexually active girls who practice contraception knowledgeably and reliably and in whom pregnancy may be considered truly accidental. There are others who are knowledgeable but inconsistent or unreliable in contraceptive use. There are pregnant girls who seemingly lack knowledge. Certainly, lack of knowledge or distortion of knowledge accounts for some teenage pregnancies. Those in girls who are intellectually handicapped are clearly included in this group.

A major role in teenage pregnancy played by our culture, unrelated to socioeconomic conditions, has been the persistent resistance to making contraceptive knowledge and means available to teenagers. Fisher and Scharf (1980) estimate that only 10 percent of pregnancies occur because the girl does not understand contraception, but 3 of 10 blamed difficulty of access to contraceptives for their failure to use them. In addition, some groups oppose birth control because of religious or political beliefs.

Kantner and Zelnik (1972) found that most girls who used contraceptives relied on the least effective methods. They also reported that one of the major reasons given by girls for failure to use protection was not that they did not know about contraceptives, but that they thought they could not become pregnant because of their age, the point in their menstrual cycle, or the infrequency of intercourse. Cobliner (1974) found that some pregnant girls had incorrect information about the efficacy or danger of certain contraceptive techniques; others had accurate knowledge but did not practice what they knew. Rogel et al. (1980) found great fear of the pill among black adolescents in Chicago, while other birth control methods were rarely thought about. The timing and source of information also can be a major factor.

While not concerned specifically with contraceptive information, Goldfarb et al. (1977) developed a predictive profile of the teenage indigent girl at highest risk for pregnancy. They found that girls most likely to become pregnant were from large families, received their sex education late and from other adolescents, and although of normal intelligence performed poorly academically or disrupted their education.

The Alan Guttmacher Institute (1985) study of teenage pregnancy, abortion, and birth rates in developed countries showed that the rate of pregnancy per year in the United States was 96 per 1,000 girls 15 to 19 years old compared with 14 in the Netherlands, 35 in Sweden, 43 in France, 44 in Canada, and 45 in England and Wales. Sexual activity rates of the girls were approximately the same among these countries, but teenagers in the United States were less likely to use contraception. It was noted that those who did were less likely to use the pill, which is considered to be the most effective method.

Giving information to adolescent girls and boys does not mean that they will acquire usable knowledge. Those teaching birth control may not be thoroughly trained or may be uneasy about imparting full information to teenagers. Dialogue with teenagers sufficient to discover and correct confusions and misunderstandings must be aimed at making sure that the students have gained the information in practical, usable form. Adolescents may state that they know about contraception without any awareness of misconceptions or gaps in their knowledge that negate the practical value of what they think they know. Cobliner (1974) and Cobliner et al. (1975) noted that effective contraceptive use by adolescent girls was possible only when they had reached the stage of formal operational thinking as described by Jean Piaget. This type of thinking permits anticipation of the consequences of behavior without having to experience the outcome. Thus, it is more difficult for sexually active early adolescents to comprehend the full impact of their sexual acting and use contraceptives effectively.

Emotional factors that contribute to teenage pregnancy have received more attention than have sociocultural or cognitive issues. Girls who become pregnant may feel more guilty about their sexual behavior, impeding their consideration of a plan for contraception. This may be coupled with a conscious or preconscious wish to become pregnant. Kane and Lachenbruch (1973) found, in addition, that pregnant teenagers show greater impulsivity, higher anxiety, and greater character disturbances than do sexually active girls who use contraceptives.

A factor that may be especially prevalent in disadvantaged groups is the sense of hopelessness about being able to control one's life and fate. Apathy and fatalism compromise the desire to avoid self-defeating behavior. MacDonald (1970) found that use of contraception may be correlated with the belief that one is able to control one's own destiny. Those who believe that their destinies are determined by forces external to themselves may fail to use contraception. Furthermore, disadvantaged girls are at greater risk when behavior that conforms with conventional values—virginity, good school performance, higher occupational goal—fails to provide tangible rewards. In these circumstances teenagers often seek self-enhancement through deviant behavior, including pregnancy (Kaplan et al., 1979). Many of the adolescent girls who become pregnant come from stressed single-parent families where fathers are not present at all.

Among the psychological factors contributing to adolescent pregnancy, Abernethy et al. (1975) found interpersonal issues crucial in the dynamics that placed adolescent girls at risk for repeated pregnancy. Their parents' marriages were characterized by distance and hostility. The girls felt alienated from their mothers and were more fond of and attracted to their fathers. Their excessive and somewhat seductive intimacy with the father excluded the mother. This pattern led to poor self-esteem as a female and to dependence on male attention and approval. The anxiety over incestuous feelings toward one's father may lead to sexual acting out with men who are substitutes for him.

Meyerowitz and Malev (1973) found attitudinal correlates among pregnant girls in a multiracial area known for high incidence of adolescent pregnancy. These attitudes were antecedent to pregnancy and significantly predictive of pregnancy risk. The three major attitudinal antecedents were (1) the belief in the external locus of control, combined with a belief in fate, hopelessness, and amorality; (2) feelings of societal rejection; and (3) a behavioral tendency toward acting out. Less predictive attitudes included apathy, desire to leave home, and passive responses to aggression. Unfortunately, attitudes are more difficult to discern than are demographic variables when trying to identify populations at risk.

Fisher and Scharf (1980) describe pregnant adolescents as variously attempting to fill an inner emptiness, to force a resolution of intergenerational dependency conflicts, to find a way to leave the parental home, and to make an abortive thrust toward mastery and individuation. Girls who become pregnant for such reasons have generally had early deficits in nurturing leading to failures in personal development and resulting in a lack of a stable sense of being a separate and worthwhile individual. They may be seeking to replace someone lost (as a dead mother), to avoid separation, or to overcome early deprivation through identification with the baby. Nadelson et al. (1980), in a study of pregnant adolescents, found that 47 percent of those in a young-mothers' clinic explicitly stated that deep down they might have wanted to get pregnant. Cobliner (1974) characterized 43 percent of his pregnant sample as risk takers without gross psychiatric disturbance. Cobliner (1981) emphasized the impact of the thrust for autonomy on the further development of the adolescent girl. He stated: "A successful loosening of the bond with the mother or maternal figure brings about a transformation of their relationship. This very relationship, a good measure of the attained level of autonomy, *seems to govern the girl's progress on the other developmental tracks, namely the social and the cognitive.* In the contrary case, the girl's development is set back and her successful adaptation is impaired" (p. 41). Copeland (1981), considering adolescents who had been pregnant only once in contrast with those repeatedly pregnant, did not find that these girls had negative self-concepts. He found some evidence of restricted personality and faulty character formation; such girls identified with their mothers, two-thirds of whom had been unmarried, pregnant teenagers.

> Mary was referred to a child guidance clinic at age 13 for promiscuous behavior and depression. Her schoolwork had been deteriorating; she reportedly had had intercourse with several classmates, and was taunted at school as a "whore." Her never-married mother had four children, each by a different man. Mary was the caretaker of the younger two and was very helpful with housework and child care.
> Mary's therapist noted that she seemed tearful and depressed and had low self-esteem. Her greatest wish was to find her real father. She believed she had never known him because he stayed away out of fear that her mother would have him arrested for failure to pay child support. Several months of supportive psychotherapy helped Mary to stop her promiscuity and to improve her peer relations. However, she interrupted therapy prematurely because of lack of funds.

Mary was next seen when she was 15 and six months pregnant. She had made an attachment to a 23-year-old truck driver and planned to marry him when she was 17. He did not feel ready to be a father, however, and abandoned her when she became pregnant.

Notman and Zilbach (1975) describe family dynamics in which there is relatively unambivalent pressure on the daughter to have a baby, exerted mainly by the mother and reinforced by other members. One such pressure arises from the mother's need to replace the lost dependency relationship with the daughter. A second is the family's need to replace a lost member, especially a sibling who died. A third is the mother's vicarious pleasure in the daughter's sexuality and the "proof" of her femaleness.

Johnson (1949) has described the effect of specific deficiencies in the moral attitudes of parents that were conveyed to their children and adolescents in a way that fostered antisocial behavior in their young even when parents themselves had not exhibited such overt antisocial actions.

Stierlin (1974) notes that rejecting and neglectful parents may push children into premature separations and a crisis runaway situation. The event of pregnancy may turn an acute crisis into one of chronic duration.

We wish to state again that adolescent pregnancy is not a syndrome and teenagers who become pregnant do not constitute a socioeconomically or psychologically homogeneous group, nor do they always show psychopathological factors. Changing societal values have diminished the stigma of out-of-wedlock births, particularly when families and society have offered economic and emotional support; some pregnant adolescent girls surmount the difficulties posed by their pregnancies and may turn this situation, just as they may all such crises, into a growth-inducing experience. Nevertheless, unmarried teenage girls seldom become pregnant for sound or emotionally healthy reasons. The pregnancy and its consequences too often lead to sociocultural and psychological impoverishment.

REFERENCES

Abernethy, V., Robbins, D., Abernethy, G.L., Grunebaum, H., & Weiss, J.L. Identification of women at risk for unwanted pregnancy. *American Journal of Psychiatry*, 132:1027–1031, 1975.

Cobliner, W.G. Pregnancy and the single adolescent girl: The role of cognitive functions. *Journal of Youth and Adolescence*, 3:17–29, 1974.

Cobliner, W.G. Prevention of adolescent pregnancy: A developmental perspective. In E.R. McAnarney & G. Stickle (Eds.), *Pregnancy and childbearing during adolescence: Research priorities for the 1980's*. March of Dimes Birth Defects Foundation. Birth Defects: Original Article Series, Volume XVII, Number 3. New York: Alan R. Liss, 1981.

Cobliner, W.G., Schulman, H., & Smith, V. Patterns of contraceptive failure. *J. Biosoc. Sci.*, 7:307–318, 1975.

Copeland, A.D. The impact of pregnancy on adolescent psychosocial development. *Adolescent Psychiatry*, 9:244–253, 1981.

Fisher, S., & Scharf, K.R. Teenage pregnancy: An anthropological, sociological, and psychological overview. *Adolescent Psychiatry*, 8:393–403, 1980.

Furstenberg, F.F., Jr. *Unplanned parenthood: The social consequences of teenage childbearing*. New York: Free Press, 1976.

Goldfarb, J.L., Mumford, D.M., Schum, D.A., Smith, P.B., Flowers, C., & Schum, C. An attempt to detect pregnancy susceptibility in indigent adolescent girls. *Journal of Youth and Adolescence*, 6(2):127–144, 1977.

Alan Guttmacher Institute. *Teenage pregnancy in developed countries: Determinants and policy implications*. New York, 1985. Also in, *Family Planning Perspectives*, 17(2):53–63, 1985.

Johnson, A.M. Sanctions for superego lacunae of adolescence. In E.R. Eissler (Ed.), *Searchlights on delinquency*. New York: International University Press, 1949, pp. 225–245.

Kane, F.J., & Lachenbruch, P.A. Adolescent pregnancy: A study of aborters and non-aborters. *American Journal of Orthopsychiatry*, 43:796–803, 1973.

Kantner, J., & Zelnik, M. Sexual experiences of young unmarried women in the U.S. *Family Planning Perspectives*, 4:9–17, 1972.

Kaplan, H.B., Smith, P.B., & Pokorny, A.D. Psychosocial antecedents of unwed motherhood among indigent adolescents. *Journal of Youth and Adolescence*, 8(2):181–207, 1979.

MacDonald, A.P. Internal-external locus of control and the practice of birth control. *Psychology Report*, 27:206, 1970.

Meyerowitz, J.H., & Malev, J.S. Pubescent attitudinal correlates antecedent to adolescent illegitimate pregnancy. *Journal of Youth and Adolescence*, 2:251–258, 1973.

Nadelson, C.C., Notman, M.T., & Gillon, J.W. Sexual knowledge and attitudes of adolescents: Relationships to contraceptive use. *Obstetrics and Gynecology*, 55:340–345, 1980.

Notman, M.T., & Zilbach, J.J. Family aspects of nonuse of contraceptives in adolescence. In H. Hirsch (Ed.), *The family. 4th International Congress of Psychosomatic Obstetrics and Gynecology.* Basel: Karger, 1975, pp. 213–217.

Rogel, M.J., Zuehlke, M.E., Petersen, A.C., Tobin-Richards, M., & Shelton, M. Contraceptive behavior in adolescence: A decision-making perspective. *Journal of Youth and Adolescence,* 9(6):491–506, 1980.

Rubin, L.B. *Words of pain.* New York: Basic Books, 1976.

Stierlin, H. *Separating parents and adolescents: A perspective on running away, schizophrenia and waywardness.* New York: Quadrangle (The New York Times Book Co.), 1974.

4
CONTEXT AND MEANING OF PREGNANCY: FATHERS

There has been a large amount of literature describing the vicissitudes of pregnant adolescent girls, but relatively little describing the adolescent boys or older males who father the pregnancies.

The high teenage pregnancy rate cannot be explained solely on the basis of high fertility or the psychology of the girls who conceive. It would be convenient to blame the problem on changes in sexual morality, breakdown of the extended family, absence of adequate contraceptive advice, or lack of effective sex education. While many of these issues are important, an understanding of illegitimate conception also requires an understanding of the psychological development and personality of the father.

A wide variety of temperamental styles and psychosocial circumstances characterize this group. Moore and Burt (1982) attempt to dispel some of the stereotypes by reviewing some recent data. For example, Scales (1977) emphasizes the fact that males have tended to be excluded from maternity-related events, although more recently there has been greater involvement of males as participants during pregnancy and childbirth. Leashore (1979) notes that males rarely have been encouraged to attend family-planning clinics, and Scales (1977) considers the level of male contraception to be surprisingly high in view of the fact that males are seldom encouraged to be involved and responsible in contraceptive techniques.

Johnson and Staples (1979) describe a sample of teenage males in the Los Angeles inner-city area who disapprove of getting girls pregnant, have generally a positive or neutral attitude toward family planning, and express a desire to learn more about birth control. A high degree of variation among young males is described by Rosenberg and Bensman (1968). They found that a group of Appalachian migrants in Chicago indicated irresponsible attitudes and double-standard values regarding pregnant cohorts. In contrast, they found in a sample of Puerto Ricans in New York and blacks in Washington, D.C. a high degree of responsibility expressed by their willingness to provide economic support and in some cases to enter a marriage contract. However, contraceptive techniques were unpopular in all three groups in this study.

Studies attempting to describe consequences of paternity to the teenage father indicate that only 10 percent of these fathers complete college by age 29, as compared to 30 percent among a matched sample of men who delayed parenthood until past 24 years of age (Card & Wise, 1978).

In terms of psychological characteristics, Rothstein (1978) found that adolescent fathers were preoccupied with different issues compared with those that concerned fathers beyond 19 years of age. The first of these was ambivalance about being a protector and provider versus being taken care of. The second theme was feelings of rivalry with one's own father. The third theme was the wide range in the measure of autonomy shown by various adolescent fathers. Rothstein did not include a control group of adolescents who had not impregnated a female. It could, therefore, be argued that the issues are common to all adolescents, adolescent fathers not representing an atypical group apart from their fatherhood.

Offer and Offer's (1974) survey of sexually active, middle-class adolescent males (not fathers) indicated that they had lower self-esteem, poorer teacher ratings, poorer psychiatric ratings, and poorer relationships with their mothers than had less sexually active and more socially conforming boys from similar backgrounds. If this were true for sexually active males, then it may also be true for adolescent fathers.

> George, 16 years old, had had the same girlfriend, Sara, for a year. Each had a private room in the basement of their respective homes, where they spent every available moment together, including much time when they were supposed to be in school. They were often not seen by their families for days at a time. George was financially indulged but severely emotionally deprived by two narcissistic, unavailable parents who had been divorced since he was five years old. He admitted to being extremely dependent on Sara, openly describing how he liked to be "mothered" by her because his mother was such a "self-centered bitch." Intercourse occurred from several times a day to once every week or two, depending on their needs for symbiotic closeness. Sara was intermittently on the pill, but his importunate infantile needs and impulsiveness led to a pregnancy when she was temporarily unprotected.

Pannor et al. (1971) did a study in a middle-class community service agency of unmarried fathers who impregnated adolescent females. Most of these fathers were not adolescents. Their median age was 22, while 28.3 percent were 19 or younger. The study reminds us that not all fathers who impregnate adolescent girls are themselves adolescents. Nevertheless, some characteristics of this group of adult and adolescent fathers were noted.

The unmarried fathers scored high in social poise, social pressure, and self-acceptance but below the norm on well-being, social maturity, and responsibility. The low score for responsibility suggested immaturity and undercontrolled impulsive behavior. The fathers also scored relatively low on scales for measuring tolerance (suggesting distrustful personal and social outlook) and intellectual efficiency (implying that the fathers lack self-direction and self-discipline). It was thought that they would use relationships for self-gratification with little concern for the needs of others.

Despite findings suggesting that adolescent fathers were irresponsible and unable to develop meaningful relationships with others, several studies (Stack, 1974; Ewer & Gibbs, 1975; Lorenzi et al., 1977; Oppel & Royston, 1971; Platts, 1968; Nettleton & Cline, 1975) noted that approximately 50 percent of teenage fathers maintain some degree of contact with the mother and infant during the first and second postnatal years. Furstenberg (1976) found that at one year following birth, nearly 90 percent of unmarried couples were still in contact. Approximately 20 percent of the mothers were married to the fathers. In Furstenberg's study 40 percent of the unmarried mothers expected to marry the fathers. Sixty percent of the males were still providing financial assistance, and 66 percent of the fathers were visiting the children on a regular basis. The level of paternal participation was not altered at a five-year follow-up even though only 20 percent of the fathers were residing with the children.

Other studies (e.g., Ewer & Gibbs, 1975; Lorenzi et al., 1977) found that the proportion of fathers actively engaged with the mother or child declined rapidly two years after the birth. Furstenberg (1976) also found that at a five-year follow-up, only 33 percent of the fathers were still providing financial assistance, and that was modest (median of $600 per year). This could be due more to the failure of medical and social services to engage the fathers than to the irresponsible attitude of the adolescent fathers themselves. Wallace et al. (1973), in a national survey of health services for teenage parents, found that only 30 percent had a component specifically designed for fathers. In fact, it often appeared that the girl's family, with the support of social agencies, actively attempted to terminate the young mother's relationship with the father out of fear that she might become pregnant by him again (Pannor et al., 1971). Furstenberg (1980) found that those adolescent fathers whose children received either their surname or first name remained significantly more involved with the children and with the mother over time. This might represent a selection factor based on a stronger prior relationship, but Pannor et al. (1971) found that fathers who were actively engaged by the social service became more significantly involved in postnatal decision making too.

Certainly, more research has to be done on the teenage-pregnancy fathers of all ages. They are often excluded from maternal-related events or family-planning clinics. The consequences of the pregnancy are different for them than for their partners. There is a paucity of knowledge about the impact of the fathers on the decisions of the mothers to abort or carry the pregnancy until birth or raise the child, about the impact of their own family of origin and peer interactions, and about the multiplicity of partners they may involve in their sexual interactions. Sexual role behavior in these adolescents and men may vary according to their culture and social class.

The studies noted here have highlighted aspects of immaturity in the psychological and social development of males who father pregnancies in adolescent girls. The studies have revealed that a number of adolescent and adult males have accepted responsible and supportive roles. The studies have not singled out a specific character type. However, the personalities of some young men who impregnate adolescent girls illustrate developmental aspects of male sexuality, particularly the role of sexual intercourse and paternity, in reinforcing a young male's sense of masculine self.

Adolescent males may assess their masculinity by comparison with male peers through athletic powers, intellectual achievement, and physical status. Comparisons include flaccid penis size, erect penis size, strength of urinary stream, and the distance of the ejaculatory spurt. Sexual intercourse may be used by some young males only to prove masculinity and potency.

To some males, potency and fertility may be equated. The more insecure the young male is about his masculinity, the more he may be driven to prove his potency to himself or others by demonstrating his ability to impregnate. A common fantasy of early and midadolescents is that a single episode of intercourse invariably leads to pregnancy. The insecure adolescent may be concerned that he is insufficiently potent. His behavior, directed toward impregnation, becomes increasingly driven by attitudes and rationalizations opposing the use of contraception. Some young males may insist that intercourse with a girl on the pill does not feel as good as when she is unprotected. The use of a condom is deplored because it interferes with sensation. Some males compare themselves with others; when one peer impregnates a girl, others are often impelled to prove themselves equally capable. In these instances the girl will have fulfilled her role and she will probably be abandoned.

There are other situations in which the boy and girl use each other in an ongoing manner as need-satisfying objects. These adolescents become intensely involved with one another, spend all their free time together, and often isolate themselves from peers and family. Their families may appear intact and functional, but youngsters involved in such intense relationships usually have experienced a variety of nurturing deficits. Such deficits make the separation and individuation of adolescence difficult or impossible, and the boy and girl solve their continuing need for infantile emotional attachments through a pseudomature heterosexual involvement. Fleck (1984) uses the term "anaclitic bondage" to describe this situation.

The young male who involves himself in this type of relationship, while he may be involved in active heterosexuality, is receiving from the girl the nurture he requires; the physical intimacy seems to fulfill the infantile needs for closeness. As well, the more that masculinity needs to be affirmed, the more coitus will be important. The more that potency must be proven, the greater the girl's risk of pregnancy.

There are some boys who are indulged materially as a substitute for receiving caring attention from parents too busy with their own pursuits. These boys grow up with the expectation that they can indulge any desire; they develop little ability to defer impulsive gratification or accept the consequences of their behavior. With girls from similar backgrounds, the combination may lead to a pattern of indulgence through promiscuous, mutually exploitative sexual activity. Even if these girls' parents actively encourage contraception, it is used unreliably. It does not require any specific personality or disturbance for ignorance, risk taking, and denial to result in pregnancy in adolescents who still manifest cognitive and emotional immaturities.

The maturation required for development of a responsible sexual relationship includes the ability to tolerate frustration without acting in such a manner as to compromise the future, to be empathic with others, to be productive vocationally, and to be able to rely on one's own creativity and imagination. These tasks are more difficult to accomplish when families and social networks do not show to then-adolescent males adult models of productive, loving mutuality. It may be more difficult for families to do so when a father is relatively absent owing to business commitments or self-indulgence and is distant and uninvolved at home, when a single-parent mother is isolated from emotionally supportive relationships and social interactions, when the father is unemployed and the mother provides the financial support, or when the family depends entirely on relatives or public assistance. Boys from such families may grow up with wariness about emotional involvements and engage in the type of superficial relationships that lead to premature pregnancy. Attempts to reduce the teenage pregnancy rate must include interventions that help adolescent boys to feel more sexually secure, to satisfy their nurturant needs more appropriately and to anticipate the consequences of their sexual behavior.

REFERENCES

Card, J.J., & Wise, L.L. Teenage mothers and teenage fathers: The impact of early childbearing on the parents' personal and professional lives. *Family Planning Perspectives*, 10:199, 1978.

Ewer, P., & Gibbs, J. Relationship with putative father and use of contraception in a population of black ghetto adolescent mothers. *Public Health Report*, 90(5):417–423, 1975.

Fleck, S. Personal communication, 1984.

Furstenberg, F.F., Jr. *Unplanned parenthood: The social consequences of teenage childbearing.* New York: Free Press, 1976.

Furstenberg, F.F., Jr. Children's names. *Journal of Family Issues*, March, 1980.

Johnson, L.B., & Staples, R.E. Fatherhood and the young minority male: A pilot project. *The Family Coordinator*, October:535–543, 1979.

Leashore, B. Human services and the unmarried father: The forgotten half. *The Family Coordinator*, October:529–534, 1979.

Lorenzi, M.E., Klerman, L.V., & Jekel, J.F. School age parents: How permanent a relationship? *Adolescence*, 45:13–22, 1977.

Moore, K., & Burt, M. *Private crisis, public cost: Policy perspectives on teenage childbearing.* Washington, DC: The Urban Institute Press, 1982, pp. 125–126.

Nettleton, C.A., & Cline, D.W. Dating patterns, sexual relationships and use of contraceptives of 700 unwed mothers during a two-year period following delivery. *Adolescence*, 37:45–57, 1975.

Offer, D., & Offer, J. Normal adolescent males: The high school and college years. *Journal of the American College Health Association*, 22(2):209–215, 1974.

Oppel, W., & Royston, A. Teenage births: Some social, psychological and physical sequelae. *American Journal of Public Health*, 61(3):751–756, 1971.

Pannor, R., Massarik, F., & Evans, B. *The unmarried father.* New York: Springer Publishing, 1971.

Platts, K. A public agency's approach to the natural father. *Child Welfare*, 47(9):530–537, 1968.

Rosenberg, B., & Bensman, J. Sexual patterns in three ethnic subcultures of an American underclass. *American Academy of Political and Social Science Annals*, 376(March):61–75, 1968.

Rothstein, A. Adolescent males, fatherhood and abortion. *Journal of Youth and Adolescence*, 7(2):203–214, 1978.

Scales, P. Males and morals: Teenage contraceptive behavior amid the double standard. *The Family Coordinator*, July, 1977.

Stack, C. *All our kin: Strategies for survival in a black community.* New York: Harper and Row, 1974.

Wallace, H.M., Gold, E.M., Goldstein, H., et al. The study of services and needs of teenage pregnant girls in the large cities of the United States. *American Journal of Public Health*, 63(1):5–16, 1973.

5
PSYCHOLOGICAL AND DEVELOPMENTAL CONSEQUENCES OF TEENAGE PREGNANCY AND PARENTHOOD

Teenage pregnancy affects the girl, the boy who impregnates her, and their families. We recognize that in adolescents an unplanned pregnancy may occur without major psychological disturbance. Ignorance, immaturity, and denial all may contribute to an unplanned, out-of-wedlock pregnancy.

It is one position of this report that teenage pregnancy in our society impairs the accomplishment of the developmental tasks of adolescence. The nature and extent of that impairment are determined by a number of factors. Some are external to the girl herself—the subcultural setting, family and social support systems, available counseling and practical assistance programs, financial and educational resources. Others are internal and relate to the girl's maturation and developmental stage, to the presence or absence of psychopathology, and to the basis of the pregnancy itself. A pregnancy occurring at an early phase of maturation and cognitive development will be perceived differently, will impinge on different developmental tasks, and will result in different consequences than one occurring during a later period of growth. Individual psychological consequences may not affect the individual alone, but through developmental arrest, pathological character formation, and maladaptive attitudes and behavior express themselves at the interpersonal level.

In like manner, socioeconomic and educational consequences affect emotions, development, character formation, attitudes, beliefs, and behavior.

Many studies have demonstrated that adolescent girls who have unwanted pregnancies are more emotionally and developmentally disturbed than even their sexually active but contraceptive-using peers. As noted in Chapter 3, Kane and Lachenbruch (1973) compared groups of pregnant and nonpregnant sexually active teenage girls using contraceptives and found that pregnant girls had more guilt over their sexual activity, had more severe acting-out character disorder, showed greater impulsivity and anxiety, and often expressed an inappropriate reaction to loss. Preexisting disturbance may motivate the willful exposure to unwanted pregnancy and the repeated experience of early pregnancy, and influence decisions about what to do about the pregnancy.

The early adolescent girl is still so psychologically tied to her mother that the meanings of pregnancy tend to reflect that relationship. Although pregnancy may be understood as a means of providing mother with a gift, pregnancy may also mean separation and loss of childhood dependency. In early and middle adolescence, a sense of rivalry may invest pregnancy with the meaning that the girl has equaled or outdone mother (Hatcher, 1973). If the pregnancy is terminated, the girl's inappropriate efforts to separate, to retain a symbolic dependency, or to resolve conflicts by threat of pregnancy will have failed. If the pregnancy is carried to term, and particularly if the girl keeps the baby, maladaptive ways of resolving immature developmental needs may become more permanently fixed, increasing the risk that the girl will remain at an immature level of ego development.

This immaturity may result in multiple pregnancies. Various studies of pregnancy repetition among teenagers strongly suggest that psychological motivation is frequently a factor. If a girl became pregnant, delivered out of wedlock in her teens, and was on welfare, she would have more out-of-wedlock deliveries during her reproductive life. In a study of 100 girls pregnant by age 15, the entire group averaged 3.4 deliveries by age 20, most of them out of wedlock, and only five girls had no repeat pregnancies by age 20 (Osofsky et al., 1973). Ignorance and immaturity may account for a number of first pregnancies, but the very fact of pregnancy could provide girls with the knowledge and means for preventing their first or further pregnancies. The high incidence of repeat pregnancies may suggest that there are psychological determinants along with social and economic factors. These girls were unable to develop beyond the level of immaturity that had made them vulnerable to an untimely pregnancy.

Early pregnancy may reinforce and corroborate a girl's sexual fears and guilt. She may be too immature to accommodate the physical changes of childbearing. Examination procedures associated with pregnancy may be perceived as traumatic events. Abortion is often poorly understood and frightening. A small number of adolescents have postabortion psychiatric sequelae. (These may include clinical depression, suicide attempts, and psychosis, but they are less common than postpartum psychiatric disorders.) Childbirth, particularly for immature girls, lends itself to confirming fantasies of genital injury. These consequences, which may seem to prove that the outcome of sexual activity is bad and damaging, can contaminate future sexual function and relationships.

With psychological disturbance or developmental deficit, the outcome is further compromised and in disturbed family relationships intensified. Girls who suffered genuine maternal deprivation often perceive a baby as someone who will give them the love they have always wanted, making up for maternal deficit. Such emotionally impaired adolescents have little resilience to cope with pregnancy and to continue their development.

The healthy adolescent girl needs to achieve separation and autonomy from her parents without excessive resentment or rebellion. This resolution normally requires years. Along the way, the teenager's partial accomplishments and the parents' cautious relinquishing of control may be tentative and shaky, but a continuous period of growth and development can be expected where there is supportive family structure.

Pregnancy can curtail this process; it can overwhelm the teenager's capacities. Pregnancy may be accompanied by fear, guilt, shame, and perhaps rage. There are always practical decisions to be made. In the current medicolegal climate, some adolescents can decide upon and obtain an abortion without parental knowledge; others are unprepared to make such a decision. Barglow and Weinstein (1973) found that the most common psychological interferences with effective abortion decision making are characteristics of normal adolescent immaturity: poor reality testing, overwhelming anxiety, failure of mental function secondary to regression, massive denial, and inability to conceptualize the future. Girls turn to their mothers not only for appropriate support and assistance but in passive and dependent defeat. The mother or both parents take over the decisions and make and carry out the plans.

This sequence of events does not necessarily indicate excessive dependency or pathogenic parental overcontrol; pregnancy makes a premature demand on the adolescent. The girl's self-confidence, her sense of being able to trust not only her judgment but also her coping ability, is undermined by a real event (Copeland, 1981). The girl and her parents find it more difficult to move away from the dependent relationship. They may be fearful, and resentful, that the girl's eventual autonomy may be compromised.

Fisher and Scharf (1980) suggest that the historical trend toward earlier menarche has added to adolescence the burden of completing the developmental tasks of latency, and precipitates girls into pseudoadult concerns, decisions, and responsibility.

The pregnant adolescent girl is confronted with the decision to abort or carry the pregnancy to term. Despite the potential physical and psychological risks of abortion to adolescents, it is, when morally and religiously possible, the least disabling choice once pregnancy exists. For that pregnancy abortion is a single, time-limited trauma. It avoids the increased sense of loss and guilt attendant upon giving an infant up for adoption after nine months of anticipatory attachment. It precludes the burdens of premature and usually single motherhood. But the very immaturity of adolescence complicates decision making. Denial may be a predominant defense in early adolescent pregnant girls, and adolescents typically delay seeking medical advice and abortion longer than do older women (Cates, 1980). Their confused body image and their equation of having a baby with confirmation of their own sexuality may override rational consideration and encourage them to resist or refuse abortion.

The type of abortion may affect psychological responses. Uterine curettage or evacuation procedures may be associated with more favorable postabortion reactions than those which mimic labor in later stages of pregnancy, but it also may be due to the fact that the pregnancy itself is of shorter duration. Adolescents tend to delay abortions until after the applicability of the simplest procedures. This may contribute to their higher rate of postabortion emotional complications, compared with older women. The delay may be indicative of the degree of conflict within the adolescent about terminating the pregnancy, a conflict that may manifest itself during the postabortion period. (Adolescents are also at higher risk than older women for postpartum psychiatric disorders.) Teenagers who carried unplanned pregnancies to term were at higher risk for psychiatric disorders than those who terminated their pregnancies (Cates, 1980). The capacity to decide on abortion correlated with a high degree of emotional maturity in a study by Kane and Lachenbruch (1973). They found that pregnant teenagers who carried their pregnancy to term showed more character disorders than those who chose abortions.

The decision for or against abortion is made more difficult for some by the view that abortion poses a serious moral dilemma. It is likely that for those who consider abortion to be murder or a mortal sin, the risks of teenage motherhood will be seen as preferable to the deed and guilt that abortion would cause. Once again, the inherent cognitive and emotional immaturity of adolescence complicates efforts to understand the various influences on decision-making processes. Some teenagers can maintain firm and lasting moral and religious convictions. The younger a pregnant girl is, however, the more likely such convictions reflect those of her family and the community rather than secure components of autonomous identity. In many adolescents these convictions can also be defenses against body image confusions, conflicts, or fantasies. Although values and beliefs often change with age and maturation, their impact may be powerful and lasting.

Some of the most obvious psychological consequences of teenage motherhood were defined by Zongker (1980). Only a minority of teenage mothers were married, and this group varied relatively little in their self-assessments from their single, nonmother peers. Single teenage mothers—the vast majority—were found to have low self-concepts, serious emotional problems, and inappropriate coping behaviors. Many saw themselves as undesirable, unworthy, and immoral; they were unhappy with their behavior, their physical selves, and their social relationships.

Because of their developmental immaturity, young adolescent girls have poor or distorted mental concepts of the fetus. Hatcher (1973) found that early adolescents conceptualized the fetus as a nonobject, an "it," and drew deadlike, unappealing, unrealistic images. Middle adolescents drew the fetus as oversized and powerful, corresponding to their fan-

Psychological and Developmental Consequences

tasy of the infant. When a pregnancy or a baby is used to express childhood needs, to substitute for the lost nurturing parent, or to accomplish separation or pseudoautonomy, it is used for purposes unrelated to the realities of motherhood or infancy. The mother is manifestly unready to engage an infant with a sense of her own real role or with empathy for the infant's real needs. While the consequences to the child are not the subject of this chapter, there are consequences to the mother. A disappointing, unfulfilling, frustrating, or even destructive experience with a first child sets the stage for repeated negative expectations and interferes with the further development necessary for the complex task of competent mothering.

> Dorothy had had chronic problems with her family and had run away for several months when she was 14 years old. When she became illegitimately pregnant and bore a daughter at 16, she was thrown out of her home. She was taken in by the baby's paternal grandmother, but was depressed and anxious over her rejection by her family. Her immaturity and the emotional problems exacerbated by the consequences of her pregnancy made her tense and artificial with her infant. Her interaction and affectionate attempts were exaggerated and intrusive, causing the baby to fuss and to try physically to avoid the mother.

Good parenting, or as termed by Winnicott (1965) "good-enough" mothering, is perhaps the most complex and demanding of all human interpersonal tasks. Infants and children are in most instances helpless against the defective handling by inadequate mothers and fathers. Teenage pregnancy tends to occur in psychologically compromised adolescents and to impair development regardless of preexisting health or disturbance. Infants will miss having their developmental needs met by mothers or fathers who are immature and in some cases psychologically damaged. The resulting defects perpetuate themselves in partial emotional development and personality organization.

Projection of guilt and responsibility is a characteristic defense of pregnant adolescents. Attitudes endure in proportion to the emotional intensity associated with their origins; unwanted pregnancy is a devastating experience regardless of how it is handled. These girls frequently have a degree of mistrust as an obstacle to overcome in future relationships with men. They rarely marry the presumed father, usually also a teenager (Copeland, 1981). When they do so and keep the baby, the resentment usually is intense and destructive to the marriage. Teenage mothers feel robbed of their adolescence, their educational possibilities, and their chances for a good life socioeconomically. Teenage motherhood and subsequent marriage escalate the risks and damaging consequences inherent in premature pregnancy. The availability of legal abortion for adolescents is associated with lower adolescent marriage rates (Cates, 1980). Finally, teenage marriages are two to three times more likely to end in divorce compared with those occurring later.

Not only the father but also the baby may be seen by the mother as the cause of the trouble. The younger the mother, the more frightening may be the experience of pregnancy and childbirth, both physically and emotionally. The infant may be seen as the tangible sign of trauma, along with the guilt and shame that may be present. The mother may be unable to form a bond with her child. Child abuse may occur. Depressive disorder is frequent; Gabrielson et al. (1970) reported a 13 percent suicide attempt rate among adolescent mothers.

While the girl may inappropriately blame others for her pregnancy, the consequences are real. For those who deliver and keep their babies, the currently increasing trend, the responsibility can be crushing. Being a full-time mother while still a teenager, especially under impoverished conditions, can result in identity foreclosure. Unless fortuitous circumstances allow subsequent growth, motherhood may limit the number of people with whom the girl can interact as a peer and may diminish the quality, breadth, and subtlety of all her interactions.

The girl for whom a baby represents her own deprived self often plans to give her child the love she believes she missed, but she may also view the baby as someone who belongs to her and will love her. Since infants are dependent, any rivalry between mother and child that leads to failure to respond to the baby's needs may result in severe feeding difficulties and a failure-to-thrive syndrome (Fraiberg, 1980). This may be intensified by the poverty level of existence of many adolescent mothers in which their own nutritional needs may be inadequately met. If the girl is married, she may focus the same insatiable needs on her husband; the baby may be seen additionally as a rival for his love.

A girl who becomes pregnant in a maladaptive effort to achieve separation from her mother may continue to cycle between infantile dependence, resentment toward the person depended upon, and disruptive efforts at separation. It will be difficult for her to help her child accomplish what she has not, and Fisher and Scharf (1980) report that such children are at particularly high risk for physical abuse. Teenage pregnancy can produce emotional damage or developmental impairment in the teenager whether or not the adolescent gives the baby up for adoption. The potential for psychiatric disturbance and developmental disruption is multiplied when a teenage girl has and keeps a baby.

REFERENCES

Barglow, P., & Weinstein, S. Therapeutic abortion during adolescence: Psychiatric observations. *Journal of Youth and Adolescence*, 2:331–342, 1973.

Cates, W. Adolescent abortions in the United States. *Journal of Adolescent Health Care*, 1:18–25, 1980.

Copeland, A.D. The impact of pregnancy on adolescent psychosocial development. *Adolescent Psychiatry*, 9:244–253, 1981.

Fisher, S.M., & Scharf, K.R. Teenage pregnancy: An anthropological, sociological and psychological overview. *Adolescent Psychiatry*, 8:393–403, 1980.

Gabrielson, I.W., Klerman, L.V., Currie, J.B., Tyler, N.C., & Jekel, J.F. Suicide attempts in a population pregnant as teen-agers. *American Journal of Public Health*, 60:2289–2301, 1970.

Hatcher, S.L. The adolescent experience of pregnancy and abortion: A developmental analysis. *Journal of Youth and Adolescence*, 2:53–102, 1973.

Fraiberg, S. (Ed.) *Clinical studies in infant mental health.* New York: Basic Books, 1980.

Kane, F.J., & Lachenbruch, P.A. Adolescent pregnancy: A study of aborters and non-aborters. *American Journal of Orthopsychiatry*, 43:796–803, 1973.

Osofsky, H.J., Osofsky, J.D., Kendall, N., & Rajan, R. Adolescents as mothers: An interdisciplinary approach to a complex problem. *Journal of Youth and Adolescence*, 2:233–249, 1973.

Winnicott, D.W. *The family and individual development.* New York: Basic Books, 1965, pp. 16–29.

Zongker, C.E. Self-concept differences between single and married school-age mothers. *Journal of Youth and Adolescence*, 9:175–184, 1980.

6
HEALTH AND SOCIOECONOMIC CONSEQUENCES OF TEENAGE PREGNANCY AND PARENTHOOD

There are substantial health risks to teenage girls during pregnancy, and these increase as the pregnancy is carried to term. With delivery, health risks extend to the child as well. In addition, socioeconomic consequences multiply health problems if the girl keeps her baby. For the boy, socioeconomic penalties accrue if he marries, remains with the girl, or tries to assume financial responsibility; in these instances the disadvantages may be almost as great for him as for the mother and child.

HEALTH CONSEQUENCES

Many of the health dangers to mother and child can be lessened through high-quality health care. Teenagers, however, those at highest health risk from pregnancy and childbirth, continue to receive the least adequate medical attention. Poor, black, rural, unmarried adolescents are most likely to be among the one-quarter of pregnant women in the United States who receive belated or no prenatal care (Select Panel for the Promotion of Child Health, 1981). The National Center for Health Statistics (NCHS, 1980a) reported that in 1978 two-thirds of the 11,000 mothers under age 15 received no care during the critical first trimester. One-fifth had no prenatal care at all or began care during the last trimester. Half of those aged 15 to 17 had no care in the first trimester, and one-eighth had no care or none until the last three months. Prenatal care for those aged 18 and 19 was comparable with that for mothers in their early twenties. Stated differently, mothers aged 15 or younger are two and one-half times more likely than mothers aged 20 to 24 to be without prenatal care in the first three months of pregnancy and nearly four times more likely to get no care at all or to delay it until the last trimester.

In addition, there is an increased incidence of obstetrical complications among adolescents. Teenage mothers are 15 percent more likely to suffer from toxemia, 92 percent more likely to have anemia, and 23 percent more likely to suffer from complications attendant upon premature birth than are mothers who give birth later (Kohl, 1978). According to unpublished data from the National Center for Health Statistics, maternal mortality is higher among teenage mothers, especially among those quite young. In 1977–78, the maternal death rate for those aged 15 and younger was 18 per 100,000 live births, two and one-half times the rate for those aged 20 to 24 (NCHS, 1980b).

As noted earlier, teenagers who obtain abortions are less likely than older women to have them in the earlier, safer weeks of pregnancy (Tietze, 1978). The younger the girl, the more likely she is to have a delayed abortion. Only 34 percent of abortions obtained by girls aged 15 or younger are performed at eight or fewer weeks' gestations, compared with 41 percent among 16- to 19-year-olds, and 51 percent of those obtained by women aged 20 to 24. At the other extreme, 14 percent of abortions obtained by the youngest group are performed at 16 weeks' gestation or later, compared with 7 percent in the middle group and 4 percent in the older group.

Statistics compiled by the National Center for Disease Control dramatize the increasing dangers associated with delay of abortion. Between 7 and 20 weeks of gestation, the risks of complications increase approximately 20 to 30 percent and the risk of death increases approximately 50 percent each week that the abortion is delayed (Cates et al., 1979). Teenagers do delay abortion; their crude death rate in 1972 was 2.2 per 100,000 procedures. In addition to death rate associated with abortion, the National Center for Disease Control reported that during the same period, teenagers as a whole showed a death rate of 9.5 per 100,000 live births. According to these figures teenagers were four times more likely to die from pregnancy continuation than from legal abortion (Cates, 1980). The death rate from continuation of pregnancy and childbirth in girls 15 years of age or younger ran at least eight times that in the remaining population of older girls and women, as reported by the National Center for Health Statistics (1980c).

The health of surviving children of adolescent parents is also adversely affected. Data from New York State show that babies of teenage mothers are nearly twice as likely to die during their first year than are babies of older mothers. Teenage mothers are more likely to have babies that are premature or of low birth weight (less than 5.5 pounds), regardless of social class (American Academy of Pediatrics, 1979); the risks are much greater for those who are poor and black. Mothers aged 15 and younger are two times more likely to have low-birth-weight infants; among all teenagers the risk is 39 percent greater. The risk declines with increasing age of the mother, but even 19-year-old mothers have rates 27 percent higher than do those in their early twenties (National Center for Health Statistics, 1980c). Many investigators suggest that the increased incidence of low-birth-weight neonates is related to competition for nutrition between the fetus and the still-growing mother (Naeye, 1981). Low birth weight has been associated with infant mortality as well as with a host of serious childhood illnesses, birth injuries, neurological defects, and mental retardation.

Much of this report thus far has been devoted to demonstrating the reasons and the ways that teenage mothers (and fathers) are developmentally unready for the complex tasks of parenthood providing the emotional nurture a child needs. It has frequently been noted that the children of adolescent parents are at higher risk to be victims of child abuse. Among the high-risk signals during pregnancy that the National Center for the Treatment of Child Abuse and Neglect (Kempe et al., 1962) has identified are: denial of the pregnancy, unwanted pregnancy, depression over the pregnancy, lack of family or social support, overwhelming anxiety in the mother, and consideration of relinquishment by the mother (Gray et al., 1977). In our view, some of these characteristics are prominent in many pregnant teenagers.

Some investigators have failed to find a simple correlation between child abuse and the age of the parents (Ory & Earp, 1978; Kinard & Klerman, 1980). In their study populations, important additional correlates with child abuse were poverty, social and family disorganization, prematurity of the infant, one-parent families, parental depression, and parental rejection. Such findings, however, do not negate the high risk for child abuse by teenage parents because teenage parenthood is more likely to occur in the presence of those additional destructive circumstances.

SOCIOECONOMIC CONSEQUENCES

Education

Statistics from the Alan Guttmacher Institute (1981) indicate that although many teenage parents finish high school and some attend college, the majority, especially young teenage mothers, never obtain a high-school diploma; of 1.1 million teenage mothers, about 670,000 have dropped out. Of women who were aged 18 or 19 when they delivered, only 18.5 percent were not high-school graduates, and less than 4 percent who delayed motherhood until age 20 had not graduated. The effect of teenage childbearing on college graduation is even greater; by age 29, women who delayed motherhood until their twenties were four to five times as likely to have completed college.

> Carla was 14 years old when she was first seen for psychiatric evaluation; her academic performance had dropped markedly and she was five months pregnant. Carla's father had abandoned the family when she was an infant, and she now lived with her mother, two older siblings, and her sister's out-of-wedlock infant daughter. The family was dependent on welfare. Carla's emotionally deprived and unsupervised early childhood helped her to find school an exciting adventure. She did well until age 13 when her sister's baby was born, when she was pressed frequently into the role of caretaker and began to miss a great deal of school. She herself soon became pregnant after a brief encounter with a teenage neighbor. Carla did not return to the clinic for two years. At the second visit she was 16, the mother of a year-old son and the chief caretaker of a three-year-old niece. She had dropped out of school and felt hopeless and depressed.

Chilman (1980) suggested from her study of the existing research that adolescent parenthood was only one factor in maternal school dropout. She wrote that teenage mothers may have tended to do poorly in school before pregnancy occurred; early marriage rather than pregnancy was more closely associated with dropping out of school. Nevertheless, the effect of early childbearing on educational opportunity is not simply the result of low aptitude, poverty, or lack of interest in learning. A national study that followed up samples of young people matched for race, socioeconomic status, academic aptitude, achievement, and educational aspirations at age 15, by Card and Wise (1978), found a disparity in educational accomplishments when this sample was reinterviewed at age 29: mothers who had given birth before they were 18 were only half as likely to have graduated from high school as were those who postponed childbearing until after they turned 20. Further evidence that teenage pregnancy is a disruptive influence in itself can be inferred from data showing that in terms of educational and occupational attainment, socioeconomically advantaged young mothers seemed to suffer greater disruption following a teenage birth compared to those who were not advantaged (Card, 1977).

For young fathers in the matched samples, the effect was less dramatic but still substantial. Those who became fathers before age 18 were less likely to have graduated from high school and college. One possible compensation for those without personal advanced educational goals is that those who entered the work force early as a result of premature high-school dropout were more likely to accrue seniority in their jobs at an earlier age than their peers who remained in school (Card, 1977).

Some studies indicate that children of teenage parents may suffer a higher incidence of cognitive and educational deficits (Baldwin & Cain, 1980). Dryfoos and Belmont (1978), after controlling for differences in socioeconomic status, race, and other variables that are correlated with both early motherhood and low cognitive scores, found a small but consistent linear relationship between lower maternal age and lower intellectual achievement by the children. The follow-up of the Furstenberg (1976) study of a small sample revealed that children of adolescent mothers had less cognitive development than did children of older mothers. Their level of attainment was related strongly to their socioeconomic background, again a legacy of the excessive youth of their mothers (parents).

As with child abuse, efforts have been made regarding cognitive status to determine the factor of teenage parenthood as a determinant of disorders. Card (1978) found, after controlling for parental variables in race, socioeconomic status, and maternal intelligence in children at the high-school level, some relationship between intellectual achievement and maternal age, particularly if the mother was under age 15. Children of adolescent parents scored lower than their classmates in all cognitive measures used, had personality traits of less sociability, maturity, and neatness, and had lower expectations for themselves. When followed up 11 years after high-school graduation, these then-adult children of adolescent parents had achieved lower final educational levels than their classmates, had married earlier, and had more divorces and subsequent remarriages.

Marriage

According to McCarthy and Menken (1979), married teenage parents were far more likely to separate or divorce than were couples whose childbearing occurred in their twenties. The trend was evident among women of all races, but was more pronounced among whites than among blacks. Forty-four percent of women who gave birth at ages 14 to 17 were separated or divorced within 15 years, three times the proportion among women who did not begin childbearing until their twenties; divorce was still twice as likely for 18- and 19-year-old mothers. The study was unable to identify the divorce rate of those couples who married during adolescence and did not become parents. These findings add to the fact that few teenage mothers ever bother to marry the putative father. In Copeland's (1981) group of 31 pregnant girls, only six intended to marry the father; none had yet carried out the intention. In the much larger study of 180 pregnant teenagers of average age 15.6 years (Lorenzi, Klerman, & Jekel, 1977), only 20 percent of the girls had married the father by two years postpartum.

As a result of this pattern, 70 percent of children born to women aged 17 or younger have spent part of their childhood in a single-parent (fatherless) household. This contrasts with 41 percent of those born to mothers who were aged 18 or 19 and 25 percent of those born to mothers in their twenties. Chilman (1980) points out that the immaturity of adolescents who marry may be a factor that contributes to the dissolution of their marriages, in addition to the stress of teenage parenting. Teenage mothers who do not marry are also more likely to return to school at some time. However, it has been found that the children of teenage mothers fare better cognitively and socially if they grow up in a two-parent home (Card, 1978).

Young mothers who do not live with the child's father are far less likely to receive child support payments from the father than are older mothers who live apart. More than one-fourth of all mothers not living with the child's father receive child support payments, whereas only one-tenth such mothers aged 14 to 24 receive support. For the small number of young mothers who do receive financial help from the fathers, the payments are minimal, averaging only $1,388 per year (Alan Guttmacher Institute, 1981).

Life-Styles, Financial Plight, and Social Cost

A 1980 report from the U.S. Bureau of the Census (1980) shows that there are nearly 600,000 families in the United States with children five years old or younger headed by single mothers aged 14 to 25. Sixty-six percent of these families are living below the officially designated poverty level. (For example, an annual income of $6,682 for a fatherless family of four is considered at poverty level.) This is five times the proportion of all families with such young children living in poverty (13 percent) and seven times the proportion of all poverty families (9 percent). The median annual income of families headed by women under age 25 is $3,953, far below the federal poverty line. Such families have incomes only one-fifth as high as average families and three-tenths as high as that of young husband-wife families.

As noted by the Alan Guttmacher Institute (1981), many teenage mothers with small children to care for, few skills, little education, and no employed husband become dependent on public welfare. In 1975, about half of the $9.4 billion invested in the Federal Aid to Families with Dependent Children (AFDC) program went to families in which the woman had given birth as a teenager (Moore, 1978). Six of ten women in families receiving AFDC payments had given birth as teenagers, contrasted with one-third of women in families not receiving such payments. Information is not currently available about how many teenage mothers are on Medicaid, on food stamps, using publicly financed services for prenatal care and delivery, and incurring public costs for needed health care and social services for themselves and their low-birth-weight infants. The total costs can be assumed to be great.

A study by Abt Associates (1979) indicates that of the 1,327,000 children with teenage mothers, only about 43,000 are enrolled in day care programs. An estimated 480,000 are taken care of by their nonworking mother, relatives, or babysitters (U.S. Bureau of the Census, 1976). Many of the remaining 804,000 children are in need of day care services, which would permit mothers who desire to do so to work or finish high school. The unavailability of child care facilities frustrates the mothers' motivation for socioeconomic improvement.

In considering the staggering documented costs—human and financial—of programs and services, it is enlightening to contrast the costs of contraceptive family planning: $66 per woman per year, or $225 million a year in terms of federal appropriation (National Family Planning Forum, 1977). In the event of unwanted pregnancy, the average total cost of suction curettage, including all pre- and postservices, is $150; procedures necessary in later stages of gestation cost approximately $300 (Cates, 1980).

Importance of the Family

The way that a girl's family responds to her pregnancy and helps her adjust to her new parenting role and responsibility influences the outcome of her untimely motherhood (Furstenberg, 1976). Teenage mothers who lived with their families during pregnancy were more likely to receive substantial amounts of financial support and child care. The great majority of these girls lived with a parent or close relative (90 percent during pregnancy, 61 percent one year after delivery, and 45 percent five years after delivery). Families were more likely to help the teenager when she remained unmarried if she continued her education, and when they were themselves a two-parent household. If she had a second pregnancy she was more likely to move out. The support provided by their families had definite long-term positive effects for both the mother and the child. Those who remained with their families were more likely to advance educationally and economically as compared with peers who left home.

These statistics probably underestimate the problem in a society in which teenage pregnancy is increasing, but they indicate the socioeconomic disaster of teenage pregnancy and what most adolescent mothers and families must face.

Furstenberg's (1976) broadly based study demonstrated that young mothers consistently experienced great difficulty in realizing life plans. A disparity existed between the goals they articulated in the first interview and their experiences following delivery. Distinct sets of problems developed with disruptions and deprivations owing to early childbearing. In contrast, their classmates who did not become pregnant premaritally had a far better record of achieving their immediate life objectives. The same study noted that one cannot conclude that parenthood in adolescence inevitably and irreversibly disrupts the life course of every female. Some hastily married the father of the child, and when these marriages were successful (rarely), the adjustment of the young mother closely resembled that of her former classmates who had delayed marriage and childbearing until their early twenties. Others, rather than marry, put off marriage indefinitely and resumed their education. When able to restrict childbearing and make child care arrangements, these women often managed to achieve economic independence by the time the study ended.

The great majority of those studied, however, were not successful in coping with the problems caused by precipitate parenthood. Prospects of achieving a stable marriage were damaged by the early pregnancy: They were having great difficulty supporting the family on their own. Poorly educated, unskilled, burdened often by several small children, many by age 21 had become resigned to a life of emotional and economic deprivation. These outcomes lead to the conclusion that teenage pregnancy and parenthood are far too frequently associated with serious biological and socioeconomic consequences.

REFERENCES

Abt Associates. *Day care centers in the U.S.* Cambridge, MA, 1979, Table 49.

American Academy of Pediatrics: Statement on teenage pregnancy. Committee on adolescence. *Pediatrics*, 63:795–797, 1979.

Baldwin, W., & Cain, V.S. The children of teenage parents. *Family Planning Perspectives*, 12:34, 1980.

Card, J.J. *Consequences of adolescent childbearing for the young parent's future personal and professional life.* American Institute for Research, P.O. Box 1113, Palo Alto, CA 94302, 1977.

Card, J.J. *Long-term consequences for children born to adolescent parents.* American Institute for Research, P.O. Box 1113, Palo Alto, CA 94302, 1978.

Card, J.J., & Wise, L.L. Teenage mothers and teenage fathers: The impact of early childbearing on the parents' personal and professional lives. *Family Planning Perspectives*, 10:199, 1978.

Cates, W. Adolescent abortions in the United States. *Journal of Adolescent Health Care*, 1:18–25, 1980.

Cates, W., Gold, J., & Selik, R.M. Regulation of abortion services—For better or worse? *New England Journal of Medicine*, 301:720–723, 1979.

Chilman, C. Social and psychological research concerning adolescent childbearing: 1970–1980. *Journal of Marriage and the Family*, 42:793–805, 1980.

Copeland, A.D. The impact of pregnancy on adolescent psychosocial development. *Adolescent Psychiatry*, 9:244–253, 1981.

Dryfoos, J., & Belmont, L. *The intellectual and behavioral status of children born to adolescent mothers.* Third Progress Report, November 30, 1977 to May 29, 1978, NICHD Contract HD-72805, 1978.

Furstenberg, F. *Unplanned parenthood: The social consequences of teenage childbearing.* New York: The Free Press, 1976.

Gray, J.D., Cutler, C.A., Dean, J.G., & Kempe, C.H. Predictions and prevention of child abuse and neglect. *Child Abuse and Neglect: The International Journal* (formerly: *International Journal on Child Abuse and Neglect),* 1:45, 1977.

Alan Guttmacher Institute. *Teenage pregnancy: The problem that hasn't gone away.* New York, 1981.

Kempe, C.H., Silverman, F.N., Steele, B.F., et al. The battered child syndrome. *Journal of American Medical Association,* 181:17–24, 1962.

Kinard, E.M., & Klerman, L.V. Teenage parenting and child abuse: Are they related? *American Journal of Orthopsychiatry,* 50(3):481–488, 1980.

Kohl, S.G. *Special tabulation for 1975–1978 data on non fatal maternal complications.* Obstetrical Statistical Cooperative, Downstate Medical Center, State University of New York, 1978.

Lorenzi, M.E., Klerman, L.V., & Jekel, J.F. School age parents: How permanent a relationship? *Adolescence,* 12:13–22, 1977.

McCarthy, J., & Menken, J. Marriage, remarriage, marital disruption and age at first birth. *Family Planning Perspectives,* 11:27, 1979.

Moore, K.A. *Testimony on the economic consequences of adolescent pregnancy and childbearing.* U.S. House of Representatives, Select Committee on Population, February 28, 1978. Washington, DC, The Urban Institute, 1978.

Naeye, R. Teenaged and pre-teenaged pregnancies: Consequences of the fetal-maternal competition for nutrients. *Pediatrics,* 67:146–150, 1981.

NCHS. Final natality statistics, 1978. *Monthly Vital Statistics Report,* 29(1), 1980a.

NCHS unpublished data. Mortality Statistics Branch, Division of Vital Statistics as stated by the Alan Guttmacher Institute, New York, 1980b.

NCHS Data Calculated from *New York State Department of Health. Quarterly Vital Statistics Review,* by the Alan Guttmacher Institute, New York, 1980c.

Ory, M., & Earp, J. The influence of teenage childbearing on child maltreatment: The role of intervening factors. Presented to the American Public Health Association, Los Angeles, California 1978.

Planned Birth. The future of the family and the quality of American life. *National Family Planning Forum,* Washington, DC, 1977.

Select Panel for the Promotion of Child Health: Report to the United States Congress and the Secretary of Health and Human Services. *Better health for our children: A national strategy.* DHHS (PHS) Publication No 7955071, 1981.

Tietze, C. *Estimates of women obtaining abortions, by age and weeks of gestation.* The Population Council, based on selected state health department reports, 1978.

U.S. Bureau of the Census. *Daytime care of children, 1975*. CPR, Series P-20, No 298, GPO, 1976.

U.S. Bureau of the Census. *Characteristics of the population below poverty level, 1978*. CPR, Series P-60, No. 124, GPO, table 19, 1980.

7
INTERVENTIONS AND RECOMMENDATIONS

Understanding the sources of a problem points the way toward solution. Every increase in knowledge is a powerful stimulus toward innovative effort and research. Some approaches have been tried with varying degrees of effectiveness; these deserve scrutiny and further study. Others show potential usefulness but have not been adequately implemented. Some potential approaches are utopian, some address society, some the family, still others the individual. Some possibilities require standard applications of social medicine. Others might seem offensive and politically explosive. The entire subject of teenage pregnancy is complicated because it combines a number of emotion-laden issues: teenage intercourse, contraception, abortion, individual rights, family integrity, societal structure.

Our approach to the problem considers both prevention of pregnancy and limitation of harmful consequences once pregnancy has occurred. What is to be prevented and what is to be minimized vary at every point from beginning sexual activity through motherhood and child rearing.

> Annette was a 16-year-old unmarried mother who was instructed by her own mother to feed her baby as much as possible to keep him healthy. As a result, her infant weighed more than 20 pounds at seven months of age, and his obesity prevented him from beginning to move about and explore his environment as babies his age would normally do. In addition, Annette felt very insecure and anxious because often

she did not know what to do when her baby was restless or cried. Her own tension led to overstimulation and agitation in the baby at a period of development when there should have been a tender and peaceful style of interaction that promotes trust and confidence in infant and mother. Thus, there was danger to both the physical and the psychological development of this child. Counseling by a social worker in a program for adolescent mothers helped Annette to resolve her anxieties. This, in turn, enabled her to accept the advice of a pediatrician that the baby should be started on a diet, which led to gradual attainment of proper weight and a normal range of activity for the infant.

At which point does prevention begin? For some it would be abstinence from intercourse; for others the focus would be on prevention of conception. If impregnation occurs, some may consider abortion; efforts to limit the consequences of the abortion become the focus. If carrying a pregnancy to term involves higher risks than termination, interruption of the pregnancy may be the way to lessen the risks. As delay in obtaining an abortion increases its dangers, facilitation would protect against maternal health hazards. If abortion is unacceptable, quality prenatal care is indicated. If keeping the baby would result in future harm to the teenage mother and her infant, efforts to encourage placing the baby for adoption would be preventive and protective. If the mother decides to keep her baby, efforts can be made to protect mother and child from many of the known hazards. Mother and child are both at risk for developmental disorder. Given one experience of pregnancy, prevention of repeat pregnancies becomes a primary concern. At each point strategies and interventions differ.

On the initial point, no influence currently known or available has succeeded in totally discouraging early intercourse. Whatever efforts have been made in our culture, there is an increasing frequency of coitus at earlier ages; girls are rapidly catching up with boys in coital experience. The potential advantages of trying to prevent pregnancy by trying to ab-

Interventions and Recommendations

stain from coitus may be offset by the possibility that when sexual intercourse does occur, the girl may not plan or know about contraception and subsequently may become pregnant.

As we noted in Chapter 2, a teenager's family can influence the levels and kinds of sexual activity in their young. Loving families that foster a secure sexual identity and sense of personal worth in their children produce adolescents who might be able and willing to defer active intercourse and would be less likely to engage in sexual activity carelessly and thus increase the possibility of pregnancy. It does not follow that such optimal rearing would actually diminish the possibility of exploratory coitus. Adolescents who feel free to experiment sexually at their own developmental pace do so with greater safety and precautions. Optimal rearing fosters the cognitive and emotional development necessary for contraceptive planning and nonexploitation of others.

There is abundant evidence that nurturing and health-fostering families can exist in the most appalling socioeconomic conditions, but deprivation and poverty impose burdens that may crush families. As shown in many studies and discussed in this report, teenagers from lower socioeconomic levels are sexually active at an early age, and their sexual activity is highly conducive to repeated teenage pregnancy and parenthood. Prevention and protection in this group require innovative socioeconomic and educational efforts.

Assuming that sexual intercourse during adolescence will occur, there are approaches that may minimize risk of pregnancy. First is accurate sexual knowledge about the body, its responses, genital functioning, and reproductive physiology. Second is contraceptive knowledge and availability of contraceptive material. It is important to clarify any distortions about harm that contraceptive devices may cause to the body. Adolescents can prevent conception when they are knowledgeable and have ready access to the best and most appropriate means. These basic requirements are of overriding importance, but the controversy and anxiety that surround birth control have prevented widespread implementation.

The simple presentation of facts through lectures or books telling adolescents how and where to obtain contraceptives may have little impact in counteracting the impulses that account for most teenage pregnancies. Sex and birth control education is most effective in circumstances or settings that foster ego development, identity consolidation, awareness of feelings, male and female communication about intimate sexual and emotional matters, and empathy. This method of sex education extends its benefits to family relationships and their development.

Many authors active in sex education report that a substantial proportion of teenagers can be taught to protect themselves and others (Osofsky et al., 1973). One of the most carefully planned and highly regarded school sex education programs (1966–69) reported that the adolescent pregnancy rate for all California was 0.9 percent, whereas for those in the programs it was 0.3 percent (Cook, 1969). Such statistics cannot in themselves prove the relationship of sex education to the lower pregnancy rate, but they do invalidate undocumented claims of those who oppose sex and contraceptive education on the grounds that discussion leads to sexual license and increased pregnancy rates. Educational programs for prevention of pregnancy among teenagers should include consideration of the already pregnant adolescent, with the educational goal of prevention of future pregnancies.

A further approach to pregnancy prevention has been to identify those girls at highest risk. Studies such as those noted in Chapter 3, of Goldfarb et al. (1977), Abernethy et al. (1975), and Meyerowitz and Malev (1973), attempt to do so. Understandably there would be social and psychological problems attendant on the selection of specific girls for special pregnancy prevention attention, but concentrated and specially designed programs could be established in selectively identified schools, neighborhood locations, or institutions serving high-risk teenage populations.

Prevention of initial or repeated pregnancy rests not only

Interventions and Recommendations   61

on educational efforts and the discovery of high-risk teenagers, but also on their utilizing the most effective contraceptive techniques—techniques that may require medical assistance and prescription, usually through the services of a clinic, agency, or private physician. The highest-risk groups are the least affluent and must use publicly funded services.

It has been argued that all such services be made available to teenagers only with parental knowledge or consent. According to the Alan Guttmacher Institute (1981), the most frequent reason given by adolescents for failing to obtain contraception, after the catchall reason of "I just didn't get around to it," was fear that parents would find out about their sexual activity—31.4 percent of noncontraceptors. The same concern contributes to teenagers' delay in abortion decision (Fielding et al., 1978). Even though it is difficult to obtain adolescents' cooperation in using contraception, many teenagers do make use of birth control practitioners and clinics, and some insist on complete confidentiality, without which they would not seek the service.

The Alan Guttmacher Institute (1985) study of teenage pregnancy in developed countries found that ready access to abortion services did not lead teenagers to have abortions, that the availability of welfare and other forms of support was not a motive for parenthood, and that greater availability of birth control and sex education did not lead to an increase in teenage pregnancy. The authors viewed sex education as a major factor affecting adolescent pregnancy, particularly when, as in Sweden, sex education emphasizes the emotional as well as the sexual components of an intimate relationship. In general, in other countries public attention was not focused on the morality of earlier sexual activity, but searched for a solution to prevent increased teenage pregnancy and childbearing. The governments saw their responsibility as the provision of contraceptive services to sexually active teenagers.

We come to the following conclusions about effective pregnancy prevention programs for teenagers:

1. Bring the programs to teenage girls and boys and their families, prior to teenage years if possible.
2. Base the program on human relations and human sexuality generally, not just on contraception.
3. Make contraception an available option if a student decides to become sexually active.
4. Provide specific information and intensive counseling for the teenagers and their families at various decision points, e.g., when deciding to become sexually active, when diagnosing the presence of pregnancy, when deciding the course of action in the event of pregnancy. Make ongoing counseling available.
5. Use a variety of media approaches to disseminate sexual educational information and to publicize programs that exist, e.g., films and tapes for discussion at school and at home.
6. Elicit the support of medical services, social services, parents, and school authorities.
7. Evaluate the program's utilization and, if possible, efficacy.

Once a girl is pregnant, she must face the pros and cons of abortion and, in addition, interventions aimed at avoiding future pregnancies. This is a difficult crisis for many teenagers; emotional conflicts may masquerade as moral issues. Professional personnel may be personally in conflict over the issue of abortion; that may influence their ability to counsel a girl objectively. Some girls will be resistant to the best abortion counseling. Nevertheless, it is appropriate to explore with the girl the psychological conflict, motivations, attitudes, values, inappropriate fears, guilt, body image distortions, medical misunderstandings, and social influence.

It is equally important to explore the role of the family of origin in its capacity to assist conflict resolution. The decision to abort or carry the pregnancy may be influenced or made

Interventions and Recommendations

by parents or one dominant parent or may be unaddressed owing to family chaos. Every effort must be made to ensure that the girl and her family and, when appropriate, the boy and his family arrive at a carefully considered decision.

If abortion is not to be considered, or is rejected, then prenatal and postnatal care must be provided for the mother and her infant. There is currently far less stigma to unwed motherhood; many teenagers with support of families and social service agencies choose to keep their babies. The decision to place the child for adoption requires careful consideration and possibly psychiatric and social services.

There are a number of adolescent girls who choose to give up their babies for adoption. Some of the girls, usually among the older adolescents, decide that for religious or personal reasons they cannot permit an abortion of their pregnancies. Others postpone or avoid considering the consequences of their pregnancies until the time for early abortion has passed. Some girls prior to delivery believe that they will keep their babies, but subsequently decide not to do so.

For all girls considering giving up their babies for adoption it is important that they have opportunity to evaluate what they want for their babies, what their babies will need, what they might and might not be able to provide for their babies were they to keep them, and what they want and need for themselves. This is particularly true for those young adolescents who think that they want to keep their babies but have little or no understanding of the consequences of doing so.

Thoughtful supportive attendance by skilled, mature counselors can be crucial in assisting the adolescent girls in making their decisions in a careful, active, and deliberate way. When these girls return to their own communities, many of them feel that they have been through a maturing experience not shared by their contemporaries. The more the girls can understand their choices and take the responsibility for them, the more their sense of maturity will have been earned.

The need for intervention programs for teenage mothers who keep their babies is well established. Although some programs provide comprehensive neonatal care, medical care, day care, parental counseling, and vocational training, most programs do not, and they have not systematically evaluated the effectiveness of their intervention. The programs should be designed to fit the particular needs of a community and should be easily accessible to young mothers. The purpose should be to establish increased awareness of the need for developmental and preventive psychological services and to build a community network for early intervention and treatment of young children and young mothers.

In their description of a comprehensive teenage pregnancy program for inner-city infants and their mothers, Salguero et al. (1980) state its importance:

> The psychological events triggered by the pregnancy ... have profound effects not only in the psychosexual development of the adolescent but also in her mothering attitudes toward her offspring. For the adolescent, who is in the midst of profound life changes before having successfully negotiated the crisis of adolescence and who is in the process of developing a sense of self, the impact of motherhood and a baby, who will soon attempt to assert his own autonomy and individuality, may prove overwhelming. (p. 404)

A comprehensive program should include interdisciplinary teams made up of physicians (pediatricians, internists, obstetricians, psychiatrists), nurses, social workers, psychologists, teachers, and community health workers. Moore and Burt (1982) have pointed out that the U.S. Congress has passed legislation (Health Services and Centers Amendments of 1978, Title VI; Public Health Service Act, Title XX—1981) recommending special services for teenage parents as follows:

1. Pregnancy testing and maternity counseling.
2. Adoption counseling and referral services that present adoption as an option for pregnant adolescents,

including referral to licensed adoption agencies in the community if the eligible grant recipient is not a licensed adoption agency.
3. Primary and preventive health services including prenatal and postnatal care.
4. Nutrition information and counseling.
5. Referral for screening and treatment of venereal disease.
6. Referral for appropriate pediatric care.
7. Educational services relating to family life and problems associated with adolescent premarital sexual relations.
8. Appropriate educational and vocational services and referral to such services.
9. Referral to licensed residential care of maternity home services.
10. Mental health services and referral to mental health services and to other appropriate physical health services.
11. Child care sufficient to enable the adolescent parent to continue education or to enter into employment.
12. Consumer education and homemaking.
13. Counseling for the immediate and extended family members of the eligible person.
14. Transportation.
15. Outreach services to families of adolescents to discourage sexual relations among unemancipated minors.
16. Family-planning services.

Intervention should begin as early as possible during the pregnancy so that optimal health care for the mother and fetus as well as psychological preparedness for the birth can occur. The need for the adolescent mother to continue her own development by means of school and job training must be addressed, as well as planning for the best available care for the infant.

Risk factors in each adolescent family must be determined. At-risk implies that the mother may be unable to provide the minimal care for her infant that is necessary for adequate development to occur. The adolescent mother is often ignorant of child care techniques, may have emotional problems, and may be anxious and overstressed by parenthood.

The intervention during the birth process is of particular importance. The young mother should have the support of a familiar team member with whom she has already had several meetings. Many of the infants born to adolescent mothers are of low birth weight and need to remain in nurseries for days or weeks. The team member may help the mother to overcome the effects of sensory deprivation frequently experienced by the isolated premature infant and help in a bonding process, which might otherwise be disturbed.

The postdelivery services provided by a teenage program can best be utilized when the introduction to the program has occurred before birth. The role of the program is to help young mothers learn parenting skills as well as meet with other young mothers in a safe and protected environment. In such a center they can share experiences and discuss personal and parenting issues. Many inner-city adolescent mothers have serious social and psychological problems; most of them do not use the conventional social and psychiatric services available in a community. The program serves as a way of helping young mothers to improve their own situation within their nuclear family and to outline personal goals. The children's needs are served when the young mother gains firsthand knowledge of the principles of child-development and learns how to help her child achieve social and cognitive skills in the day care setting provided by the program.

One group of pregnant teenage girls that undoubtedly should come to the attention of psychiatrists consists of individuals with severe psychiatric disorder who have been hospitalized. These girls, their families, the fathers of their pregnancies, and the families of those fathers must be given at least as much individualized support and services as is given to others, notwithstanding the presence of a hospital staff, which may have its own biases or convictions regarding interventions. For hospitalized potential mothers and fathers family planning counseling services should be provided.

REFERENCES

Abernethy, V., Robbins, D., Abernethy, G.L., Grunebaum, H., & Weiss, J.L. Identification of women at risk for unwanted pregnancy. *American Journal of Psychiatry,* 132:1027–1031, 1975.

Cook, P.W. Memo to Board of Trustees, Anaheim Union School District, Anaheim, CA, April 24, 1969.

Fielding, W.L., Sachtleben, M.R., Friedman, L.M., & Friedman, E.A. Comparisons of women seeking early and late abortion. *American Journal of Obstetrics and Gynecology,* 131:304–310, 1978.

Goldfarb, J.L., Mumford, D.M., Schum, D.A., Smith, P.B., Flowers, C., & Schum, C. An attempt to detect pregnancy susceptibility in indigent adolescent girls. *Journal of Youth and Adolescence,* 6(2):127–144, 1977.

Alan Guttmacher Institute. *Teenage pregnancy: The problem that hasn't gone away.* New York, 1981.

Alan Guttmacher Institute. *Teenage pregnancy in developed countries: Determinants and policy implications.* New York, 1985. Also in *Family Planning Perspectives,* 17(2):53–63, 1985.

Meyerowitz, J.H., & Malev, J.S. Pubescent attitudinal correlates antecedent to adolescent illigitimate pregnancy. *Journal of Youth and Adolescence,* 2:251–258, 1973.

Moore, K., & Burt, M. *Private crisis, public cost: Policy perspectives on teenage childbearing.* Washington, DC: The Urban Institute Press, 1982.

Osofsky, H.J., Osofsky, J.D., Kendall, N., & Rajan, R. Adolescents as mothers: An interdisciplinary approach to a complex problem. *Journal of Youth and Adolescence,* 2:233–249, 1973.

Salguero, C., Yearwood, E., & Schlesinger, N. Studies of infants at risk and their adolescent mothers. *Adolescent Psychiatry,* 8:404–421, Chicago: University of Chicago Press, 1980.

8
SUMMARY AND CONCLUSIONS

In the introduction to this report, we stated that adolescents trouble adults. That is certainly true. It is equally true that many adolescents today are troubled, and when pregnant, are troubled in ways that endanger their own development, the development of the children whom they may bear, and society as a whole.

We have to set forth the severity and dimension of the problem of adolescent pregnancy. We have considered biological, psychological, and social aspects of adolescent sexuality. We have discussed characteristics of girls at risk for pregnancy and of males who become fathers. We have described consequences of adolescent pregnancy and possible health-oriented interventions.

We have emphasized the importance, albeit not exclusive importance, of the psychological factors involved in adolescent pregnancy. Some of the theoretical and clinical comments have been based on individual cases that may not always be representative of this group but have demonstrated the heterogeneity of factors and the multiplicity of variables that must be assessed by the clinician.

The differences in personality and character structure, the perceived levels of psychological and sexual satisfaction in these adolescent couples, the impact of developmental progression, and the adolescents' coping strengths and vulnerabilities should be some of the psychological variables submitted to the rigors of research and correlated with the biological and social aspects of this population. Perhaps then risk factors may emerge that will identify and facilitate better preventive and treatment approaches.

We conclude that efforts toward prevention through education and family involvement are primary, that for the pregnant adolescent girl, abortion, if acceptable, is the least disabling choice, and that the potential for physical illness, psychopathology, and developmental disruption is multiplied and extended to the next generation when an adolescent girl delivers and keeps her baby.

Our considerations of the problems and consequences of each step from conception through child rearing have confirmed our concern that adolescent pregnancy presents a crisis in development to our youth. It constitutes a crisis in our society and a challenge to provide continued help for those who must be learning to help themselves and others. It presents a crisis for those to be born; their optimal development is in jeopardy. It presents a crisis for all of us. It demands our attention.

APPENDIX: PROGRAMS FOR HIGH-RISK ADOLESCENT MOTHERS AND THEIR INFANTS

The need for intervention programs for teenage mothers is well established (Niswander & Gordon, 1972; Klerman & Jekel, 1973; Salguero et al., 1980; Kochen, 1982). The programs should provide comprehensive neonatal care, medical care, day care, parental counseling, and vocational training. They should be designed to fit the particular needs of a community. The purpose should be to establish increased awareness of the need for developmental and preventive psychological services as well as to build a community network for early intervention and treatment of young children and young mothers.

Programs must provide continuity of care and develop a strong outreach component. The following components should be an integral part of any program.

1. Identification of the population at risk.
2. Establishment of linkages to community support systems with referral for specific therapeutic interventions when necessary.
3. Continuous support for young parents of children from birth to age three.

The program should have the potential to demonstrate that adolescents who become parents can still be helped to complete their own development while at the same time learning to meet the needs of their children. Early intervention can detect and alleviate developmental problems before they lead to lasting psychiatric sequelae; the potential for child abuse can be minimized as adolescents learn to cope with parenthood while completing their own development as mature adults. Many young women are unable to provide minimal care for their infants so that adequate development may occur. The young mother is often ignorant of child care techniques; she may have emotional problems and may be anxious and overstressed by parenthood.

MODEL PROGRAM FOR HIGH-RISK ADOLESCENT MOTHERS

The program to be described as a model teenage pregnancy program is a composite of several excellent programs in existence at the present time. A program should be especially designed to meet the needs of the particular community it serves. The following program would be appropriate for a large urban hospital center with community involvement.

The major program components are:

- A. Primary prevention of adolescent pregnancy.
- B. Pre- and postnatal services for the pregnant adolescent.
- C. Parent-child center for comprehensive services for adolescent parents and their mothers.
- D. Data collection for research and training.

A. Primary Prevention Program

The adolescent population is referred from departments of pediatrics and adolescent medicine, local high schools, social agencies, clergy, and individual families. Teenage girls and boys aged from 13 to 18 are invited to participate in an adolescent afterschool program that includes creative arts, sports, and weekly "rap sessions" conducted by professional mental health workers. During the course of the year various professionals such as nurses, physicians, and counselors are invited to provide education on such issues as sexuality, the reproductive system, contraception, venereal disease, and sexual and social responsibility. The girls are offered referrals to the gynecology clinic for gynecological examination,

Appendix

contraceptive information, and services. Parent groups are an integral part of the adolescent afterschool program; they meet monthly with members of the professional staff to discuss ways of dealing with their teenage children about sexuality, drug and alcohol abuse, and planning for future work.

B. Pre- and Postnatal Services for Pregnant Adolescents

Once a sexually active teenager becomes pregnant, she is referred to the obstetrics-gynecology department for pregnancy testing and maternity counseling. Abortion counseling is provided as well. Educational services concerned with nutrition, drug use during pregnancy, and referral services for adoption are offered to those teenagers who plan to remain pregnant until delivery. For some girls who decide to keep their babies social services are provided for the adolescent mother so that she can continue school and job training. The young mother is helped to make decisions about the primary caretaker—grandmother or extended family if there is no father available for actively sharing in child care duties.

Referral is made to the parent-child center. A member of the center staff visits the pregnant adolescent during the third trimester and a few days after delivery. Arrangements are made for several home visits by the parent-child staff.

C. Program for Adolescent Mothers

The parent-child center is a model program designed to meet the psychological, and social, needs of the mother, infant, and members of the extended family. The establishment of linkages to other resources—medical, including psychiatric, educational, social—is an integral part of the program. One individual primary worker is assigned to a mother-child dyad; it is assumed that the same primary worker should remain in that role for the duration of service provided. One of the program's chief goals is to establish increased awareness of the need for developmental and preventive psychological services as well as to build a community network for early identification and treatment of young mothers and their infants. The following services are available for adolescents:

1. Parenting education groups, for adolescent mothers and fathers.
2. Individual and group psychotherapy.
3. Counseling for parents of adolescent mothers (grandparents).
4. Mother-child interaction groups.
5. Developmental testing of children.

The services are supplemented by home visits for the purpose of ongoing assessment and for counseling in intervention. The home-visiting program is staffed by paraprofessionals or college students under the supervision of senior staff.

The program is housed in a large apartment adjacent to the hospital, which contains a playroom, conference rooms, kitchen, bathroom, and offices. The atmosphere is homelike and nonclinical. One room has been converted into a small videotape laboratory for research and training purposes.

The program is specifically an "umbrella" program, designed to meet the needs of the teenage parent, and provides coordinated and comprehensive care for the adolescent mother that extends into the early years of her child's life. The program components include a multidisciplinary team, an administrative unit, and a demonstration clinic. This program is directed by a child and adolescent psychiatrist and includes a coordinator, social worker, developmental psychologist, pediatrician, nurse-practitioner, and secretary.

Teenage mothers' group. The mothers who attend the group are from extremely deprived social environments. The mothers, who bring their children, attend a weekly meeting that lasts about 2½ hours. The session consists of a group session with a counselor, which lasts 1 to 1½ hours, and discussions by the mothers in smaller groups alone for one hour. The

Appendix

goals of the group are to help the mothers begin to understand their own dependency needs and their relationships with their own families and to take some realistic steps toward their own development. These may include continued formal education.

Father's group. Fathers are encouraged to participate in the program. In addition, a weekly group session is provided specifically for them. The goal is to help them with their abilities in relationship to the mother and to the children.

Babies' and children's groups. While the mothers are participating in the group therapy session, the babies are seen separately in an adjacent playroom staffed by a developmental psychologist, a mental health worker, and two student volunteers. A play group is conducted where older children receive help in play and in interaction with peers. Ongoing observation of the babies takes place weekly, and individual attention is given to the children who are in need of one-to-one relationships.

Day program for mothers and babies—Mother-child interaction. Mothers and their children up to three to four years of age are able to participate in a three-hour program held twice a week at the parent center. Mothers are free to stay with their children or to leave them with our staff for the duration of the meeting.

This program is geared toward babies from the first months of life and toddlers. Full day care services are provided. The focus of this program is to foster adaptive mother-child interaction. Full clinical and developmental evaluations of the children are done in the context of the day program. This includes a follow-up of their progress.

Mothers' luncheon group. This group meets once a week for a period of two hours in which the mothers prepare and serve a luncheon for themselves and their children with the help of the staff. In this milieu the mothers are supported in their role as caretakers.

Individual treatment. Some of the mothers and fathers may need psychiatric intervention, which is made available as needed.

Outreach in the parent-child program. Mothers and babies who most need the program frequently do not trust hospital workers, clinics, or social services. Therefore, a home-visiting program for mothers and babies is available. Families are visited once a week on a regular basis.

D. Data Collection for Research and Training

The program should be able to serve as a demonstration clinic for research and training purposes. Maternal behavior assessment instruments and tools to evaluate the mother-child relationship should be developed.

The program should be used to train mental health professionals and paraprofessionals in parenting skills and primary prevention of developmental problems.

REFERENCES

Klerman, L.V., & Jekel, J.F. *School-age mothers: Problems and policy.* Hamden: The Shoe-String Press, 1973.

Kochen, I. *The parent-child center: A program for adolescent mothers and their families. Program description.* St. Luke's–Roosevelt Hospital Center. St. Luke's Site. New York City, NY, 1982.

Niswander, K.R., & Gordon, M. The women and their pregnancies. *The Collaborative Perinatal Study of the National Institute of Neurological Diseases and Stroke.* Philadelphia: W.B. Saunders, 1972.

Salguero, C., Yearwood, E., & Schlesinger, N. Studies of infants at risk and their adolescent mothers. *Adolescent Psychiatry,* 88:404–421.

INDEX

Abernethy, G.L., 19, 60
Abernethy, V., 19, 60
Abortion, 5, 35–38, 58
    costs of, 51
    counseling and, 62–63, 73
    father's influence on, 29
    health risk and, 44–45
    as the least disabling choice, 70
    lower marriage rates and, 40
    parents' consent and, 61
Abt Associates, 51
Acting-out behavior, 19, 34
Adolescent boys
    fantasies about pregnancy, 12
    masculinity and, 29–30
    sexually active, 26–27
Adolescent fathers, 25–31
    education, 48
    groups for, 75
    psychological characteristics of, 26–27
Adolescent girls
    fantasies about pregnancy, 11–12
    at highest risk for teen pregnancy, 60
    mother/daughter relationship, 34–35
    self-concept and, 8
Adolescent mothers, 15–21
    ability to mother infants, 39–41
    concept of the fetus, 38
    education and, 46–48
    family response to, 51–52
    groups for, 74–75
    intervention programs for, 63–67, 72–76
    model program for, 73–76
    mortality, 44–45
    mother/child interaction, 75
    poverty and, 3–4, 50–51
    with psychiatric disorders, 66–67
    at risk, 66
    suicide attempt rate, 40
Adolescents, xvii–xviii, *see also* Teenage pregnancy
    cognitive development, 7–8
    developmental crisis and, xviii–xix
    impaired developmental tasks of, 33–34
    sexual development, 8–9
    sexually active, 3, 9–10, 26–27, 59
Adoption, 3, 37, 58, 63–65, 73
Aggression, 9
Aid to Families with Dependent Children (AFDC), 51
Alan Guttmacher Institute, 3, 17, 46, 50, 61
Alcohol abuse, 4
Anaclitic bondage, 30
Anemia, 44
Anxiety, 18, 34
    abortion and, 36
    child abuse and, 46
Apathy, 18–19
Autonomy, 7, 11, 20, 26, *see also* Separation/individuation
    in healthy adolescent girls, 35–36

Babies, *see* Infants
Baldwin, W., 48
Barglow, P., 36
Bell, R.R., 10
Belmont, L., 48
Bensman, J., 26
Birth control, *see* Contraception
Black adolescents, sexually active, 10
Body image, 37–38
Burt, M., 25, 64

Cain, V.S., 48
Card, J.J., 26, 47–48, 50
Cates, W., 37, 40, 45, 51
Character disorders, 39
Character disturbances, 18
Child abuse, 40–41, 46
    intervention programs for, 71
Child support payments, 50
Childbirth
    fantasies of genital injury and, 35
    fears concerning, 12
Children (of teenage parents), 48–49, 75, *see also* Infants

Chilman, C., 10, 47, 49
Cline, D.W., 28
Cobliner, W.G., 17–18, 20
Cognitive development, 7–8
　children of adolescent mothers and, 48–49
Contraception, 16–18, 31, 34
　availability, 62
　males and, 25–26, 30
　parents' consent and, 61
　primary prevention program and, 72–73
　repeated pregnancies and, 61
　sex education and, 59–60
Cook, P.W., 60
Copeland, A.D., 20, 36, 40, 49
Coughey, K., 10
Counseling
　for abortions, 62, 73
　for adoption, 63–65
Culture, 5
Currie, J.B. (Gabrielson), 40
Cutler, C.A. (Gray), 46

Data collection, 76
Day care programs, 51, 75
Dean, J.G. (Gray), 46
Defenses, 40
Denial
　abortion and, 36–37
　of the pregnancy, 46
Depression, 40
　child abuse and, 46
　postabortion, 35
Developmental arrest, 33
Developmental crisis, xviii–xix
Developmental problems, 71
Divorce, 40, 49, *see also* Marriage
Double-standard values, 26
Drug abuse, xviii, 4, 73
Dryfoos, J., 48

Earp, J., 54
Education, 16–17, 46–49, *see also* Sex education
　for parenting, 74
　of teenage fathers, 26
Ego development, 34, 60
Environmental deprivation, 4
Evans, B. (Pannor), 27–29
Ewer, P., 28

Failure-to-thrive syndrome, 41
Families, 51–52
　influence on teen sexual activity, 19, 21, 59
　single-parent, 19, 31, 46, 49–51
Family-planning, 65
　clinics, 25
　costs of, 51
Father, as a model, 31, *see also* Adolescent fathers
Fertility, 30
Fetus, *see* Infants; Prenatal care
Fielding, W.L., 61
Fisher, S.M., 3, 16, 19, 36, 41
Fleck, S., 30
Flowers, C. (Goldfarb), 17, 60
Friedman, E.A. (Fielding), 61
Friedman, L.M. (Fielding), 61
Frustration tolerance, 31
Furstenberg, F.F., 16, 28–29, 48, 52

Gabrielson, I.W., 40
Gender identity, 7
Gibbs, J., 28
Gilligan, C., 7
Gillon, J.W. (Nadelson), 20
Gold, E.M. (Wallace), 28
Gold, J. (Cates), 45
Goldfarb, J.L., 17, 60
Goldstein, H. (Wallace), 28
Gordon, M., 71
Gray, J.D., 46
Grunebaum, H. (Abernethy), 19, 60
Guilt, 9, 18, 34–35, 40
　abortion and, 37–38

Hatcher, S.L., 34, 38
Health risks, 43–46
Health services, 28
Health Services and Centers Amendments of 1978, Title VI, 64
High-school dropouts, 46–47
Home-visiting program, 74, 76
Hopelessness, 18–19

Identity consolidation, 60
Identity, gender, 7
Immaturity, xviii, 34–38
　adolescent fathers and, 29
　adolescent marriage and, 49–50
Impulse gratification, 31
Impulsivity, 18, 34

Index

Incestuous fantasies, 9, 19
Individual therapy, 75–76
Individuation, *see* Separation/individuation
Infants
    adolescent mothers' ability to care for, 39–41
    failure-to-thrive syndrome and, 41
    groups for, 75
    health risks, 5, 45
    low birth weight, 66
    mortality, 45
    premature, 44–46, 66
    used to make up for maternal deficits, 35, 41
Intellectual achievement, 48–49
Intellectual efficiency, 27
Intercourse, premarital, 9–10, 15–16
Intergenerational dependency conflicts, 19
Intervention programs, model program, 72–76

Jekel, J.F., 28, 40, 49, 71
Jessor, R., 10
Jessor, S.L., 10
Johnson, A.M., 21
Johnson, L.B., 26

Kane, F.J., 18, 34, 37
Kantner, J.F., 10
Kaplan, H.B., 19
Kempe, C.H., 46
Kendall, N. (Osofsky), 35, 60
Kestenbaum, C.J., 9
Kinard, E.M., 46
Klerman, L.V., 28, 40, 46, 49, 71
Kochen, I., 71
Kohl, S.G., 44

Lachenbruch, P.A., 18, 34, 37
Leashore, B., 25
Lorenzi, M.E., 28, 49
Loss, inappropriate reaction to, 34
Low birth weight, 45, 66

MacDonald, A.P., 18
Malev, J.S., 19, 60
Marriage, 15, 40, 49–50, 52
Masculinity, 29–30
Massarik, F. (Pannor), 27–29
Masturbation, 8–9

Maternal mortality, 44–45
McCarthy, J., 49
Menarche, 8, 36
Menken, J., 49
Mental retardation, 45
Meyerowitz, J.H., 19, 60
Moore, K., 25, 51, 64
Moral values, 8
Mothers, *see* Adolescent mothers
Mothers' luncheon group, 75
Multidisciplinary team approach, 74
Mumford, D.M. (Goldfarb), 17, 60

Nadelson, C.C., 20
Nettleton, C.A., 28
Nishwander, K.R., 71
Notman, M.T., 20–21
Nutrition, 4, 41, 65, 73
    low birth weight infants and, 45

Object relations, 30
Obstetrical complications, 44
Offer, D., 26
Offer, J., 26
Oppel, W., 28
Ory, M., 46
Osofsky, H.J., 35, 60
Osofsky, J.D., 35, 60
Outreach programs, 76

Pannor, R., 27–29
Parenting education, 74
Paternity, *see* Adolescent fathers
Pathological character formation, 33
Petersen, A.C. (Rogel), 17
Physical abuse, 40–41, 46, 71
Piaget, J., 18
Pill, birth control, 17, 30
Platts, K., 28
Play groups, 75
Pokorny, A.D. (Kaplan), 19
Postabortion psychiatric sequelae, 35, 37
Postdelivery services, 66
Postpartum psychiatric disorders, 37
Potency, 29–30
Poverty, 3–4, 16
    child abuse and, 46
    failure-to-thrive syndrome and, 41
    single-parent families and, 50–51
Pregnancy, *see* Teenage pregnancy
Premarital intercourse, 9–10, 15–16

Premature infants, 44–46, 66
Prenatal care, 43–44, 58, 63, 65
　model program for, 73
Prevention programs, 70
　to discourage early intercourse,
　　58–59
　identifying girls at risk, 60
　to minimize risk of pregnancy,
　　59–60
　primary, 72–73
　repeated pregnancies and, 60-61
Projection of guilt, 40
Psychiatric disorders, 66–67
Psychosis, postabortion, 35
Psychotherapy, 74
Puberty, xviii, 8
　masturbation and, 9
Public Health Service Act, Title XX, 64

Rajan, R. (Osofsky), 35, 60
Reality testing, 36
Regression, 36
Research, 76
Rivalry, 34, 41
Robbins, D. (Abernethy), 19, 60
Rogel, M.J., 17
Rosenberg, B., 26
Rothstein, A., 26
Royston, A., 28
Rubin, L.B., 15

Sachtleben, M.R. (Fielding), 61
Salguero, C., 64, 71
Scales, P., 25
Scharf, K.R., 3, 16, 19, 36, 41
Schlesinger, N. (Salguero), 64, 71
School dropouts, 46–47
Schools, 16
Schulman, H. (Cobliner), 18
Schum, C. (Goldfarb), 17, 60
Schum, D.A. (Goldfarb), 17, 60
Self-concept, 8
Self-defeating behavior, 18
Self-esteem, 9, 19, 27
Self-gratification, 28
Selik, R.M. (Cates), 45
Separation/individuation, 19–20, 30, *see also* Autonomy
　baby used to express, 39–40
　in healthy adolescent girls, 35–36

Sex education, 17–18, 25, 59–62, 65
　primary prevention program and,
　　72–73
Sexual activity, adolescent, 3, 9–10,
　26–27, 59
Sexual development, 8–9
Sexual fears, 35
Sexual role behavior, 29
Shelton, M. (Rogel), 23
Silverman, F.N. (Kempe), 46
Single-parent families, 19, 31, 49
　child abuse and, 46
　poverty and, 50–51
Smith, P.B., 19, 22, 60
Smith, V. (Cobliner), 18
Socioeconomic deprivation, 16, 53
Stack, C., 28
Staples, R.E., 26
Steele, B.F. (Kempe), 46
Stierlin, H., 21
Suicide attempts, xviii, 40
　postabortion, 35

Teenage pregnancy, *see also* Headings
　beginning with "Adolescent"
　biological complications of, 5
　child abuse and, 46
　contraceptive knowledge and, 16–18
　as an emotion-laden issue, 57
　emotional factors conducive to,
　　18–19
　emotional/economic deprivation and,
　　16, 53
　family dynamics conducive to, 19,
　　21, 51–52, 59
　girls' fears concerning, 12
　health consequences of, 43–46
　intervention programs for, 63–67
　modern industrial technological
　　culture and, 5
　number in developed countries, 17
　number in the U.S., 3
　prevention programs, 58–62, 70,
　　72–73
　psychological consequences of, 64, 69
　psychological factors conducive to,
　　19–20
　psychological significance of, 11–12
　repetition of, 34–35, 60–61
　sociocultural factors conducive to,
　　15–16

Index

socioeconomic consequences of, 46–53
Therapy, individual, 75–76
Tietze, C., 44
Tobin-Richards, M. (Rogel), 17
Toxemia, 44
Tyler, N.C. (Gabrielson), 40

Unemployment, 16
Uterine curettage, 37

Values, xvii–xviii, 26
Venereal disease, 65, 72
Vocational services, 65, 71

Wallace, H.M., 28
Weinstein, S., 36
Weiss, J.L. (Abernethy), 19, 60
Welfare, 4, 34, 50–51
White adolescents, sexually active, 10
Winnicott, D.W., 39
Wise, L.L., 26, 47

Yearwood, E. (Salguero), 64, 71

Zelnik, M., 10
Zilbach, J.J., 21
Zongker, C.E., 38
Zuehlke, M.E. (Rogel), 17